Anthony Babb BEM

Operation Argentina

Falklands Museum, Rattenbach Report & Memorials 2020

Cover Photograph: Falklands Museum in Buenos Aires
Background: Pale Maiden, Falklands Official Flower
taken on Mount Tumbledown

First published in 2020 by Anthony Babb BEM
Copyright © Anthony Babb BEM

Anthony Babb BEM asserts his right under the Copyright, Design and Act 1988 to be identified as the author of this work.

All rights reserved. No part of this publication may be reproduced, stored, or transmitted in any form, or by any means, electronic, mechanical or photocopying, recording or otherwise, without the express permission of the publisher.

ISBN: 9798648360990

The author made every effort to ensure the accuracy of the information in this book at the time of going to press.
However, he cannot accept any responsibility for any loss, injury or inconvenience resulting from the use of the information contained in this book.

This book is sold subject to the condition that it shall not, by way of trade or otherwise, be lent, resold, hired out or otherwise circulated without the publisher's prior consent in any form of binding or cover than that in which it is published and without a similar condition, including this condition, being imposed on the subsequent purchaser.

Contents

Introduction 4
A lucky meeting 8
Arrival in Buenos Aires 9
The Museum at last and the Belgrano 14
Museum Layout 21
ZAMBA's AMAZING EXCURSION (Z) 23
FALKLANDS TIMELINE (P) 25
TEMPORARY EXHIBIT (1) 50
GEOGRAPHY, FLORA AND FAUNA (2) 63
RAYMUNDO GLEYZER (3) 67
ROOM (4) 68
BIOGRAPHIES (5) 81
THE 3 PLAZAS (6) 86
ROOM (7) 89
MEDIA SECTION (8) 96
Museum Review 97
Review of the Rattenbach Report 99
Puerto Madryn 125
Ushuaia 134
Author's other books 138
The Author 140

Introduction

The Falkland War defined my 23-year naval career as a Weapons Systems Engineer. I know that the purists would call it a conflict but I don't, that is my choice.

Three shipmates that I trained with in 1964 did not return, one on HMS Sheffield and two on HMS Coventry, all doing the same job I did on that type of ship (a Type 42). I served for 4 years on HMS Sheffield from build with the task force commander Sandy Woodward as my Captain in 1977; to me, he was a good choice. Initially, when I first met him he was very direct, almost intimidating however I soon realised that he was just extremely focussed. He expected you to do your job and did not suffer fools gladly but he cared for his crew, he just didn't show it.

At the time of the Argentinian Invasion in 1982, I was serving on HMS Southampton which was the latest Type 42 to join the fleet. We were still doing our trials and were not ready for war but when the call came we were ready in 4 weeks. This included 2 weeks war training with our first Seadart missile firing in the middle weekend and then 2 weeks in Portsmouth dockyard being modified, because of all the lessons being learnt down south. We even found time to investigate and help fix a Seadart software fault reported by HMS Exeter. Between other jobs, I manufactured some General Purpose Machine Gun deck mounts because we had given ours to the Task Force in April.

At the end of this stressful time Operation Corporate despatched us to the Falklands for 4 months, the "Navy News" nicknamed us the Force after the Force. I did not set foot on land until we got back and the 102 days in defence watches was not pleasant but at least no one attacked us; that I cannot imagine.

We were to go again in 1983 with Sam Salt as our Captain for a similar period; he had been the Captain of HMS Sheffield when she was sunk. Many other warships did the same whilst the Falkland defence was sorted out with the building of Mount Pleasant Airbase and radar installations. Again it was mostly a working trip but I did manage 3 hours ashore in San Carlos and 3 hours in Stanley, it was winter but I loved the place.

During a short voyage to South Georgia we paid our respects to HMS Sheffield, we had quite a few survivors on board. During this trip Sam Salt gained my respect as a Captain, he was not the same as Sandy, he was a man of the people but both were very good Captains, just different.

Sir John Holmes carried out a medal review in 2012 and from this, I was awarded the South Atlantic Medal without rosette, we may not have fought in 1982 but we were prepared and HMS Southampton was the first warship to patrol west of the Falklands. I feel lucky that I did not have to fight and great respect for those that did but I wear my medal with pride.

Before I received my medal we had already booked a cruise around South America on P & O Arcadia in 2013. They had planned visits to 3 Argentinian ports and The Falklands. Unfortunately, this was the time when the politicians in Argentina threatened to ban British cruise ships or impound them.

The cruise schedule was changed to remove Argentina from the itinerary and keep our visit to the islands. Bad weather in Stanley (wind) cancelled that call and my hopes and the hopes of many others on board of a visit were dashed. Luckily in 2015 I visited The Falklands for almost 2 weeks as a 1982 veteran and learnt so much about this far place, cemented my love for it and satisfied my deep wish to revisit.

Following that stay, I wrote my Falklands re-visited talk, much of it about the fantastic wildlife, a little about the war but also the history of the islands. I had spent a complete day in the Falkland Island Museum which is outstanding. The displays and material inside are top class and I was told by the staff that they needed bigger premises because a huge amount of material, especially 1982 matter was in storage, I added to their problems by handing over some artefacts I had from my naval career, items from my time on HMS Sheffield and an article written by Sam Salt in our ships newsletter about his first impressions on returning to see them. Remember he did not see the Falklands in 1982. It is a beautifully written piece and brought a tear to their eyes as they read it. Sam wanted the islands to remain British and he loved the place with all its wildlife and wonderful people.

Research at home on the history of the islands revealed a fragmented picture of claim and counterclaim about sovereignty but what was clear to me was that the island has been settled by some unique people who are more British than I am. They deserve the right to remain as they wish and that was what was fought for in 1982. It is the people not the place that matters and at least the United Nations agree with that. As part of my talk, I mention that the people of Argentina are taught at school that the Falklands belong to them, I was pretty certain that this was correct but it was impossible to find any details.

Then in 2020, we booked another South America round trip but this time on Cunard's Queen Victoria and this would include the 3 lost Argentinian port visits of 2013. Surely there would be an opportunity to add to my knowledge of Island history and perhaps add an Argentine view, well that was my hope.

We had planned visits at each port to see the country but I also wished to get more of an understanding of the Argentinian view about 1982. Talking to the locals was unlikely to be an option but, I discovered that there are 1982 memorials in Buenos Aires, Puerto Madryn and Ushuaia. Added to that there is a Museum in the capital that is free to enter. Provided I could get there safely, I hoped to find out what the Argentinian people are being told, they built this museum and it should reflect the view of the nation.

Here you will find the story of my clandestine visit to the Museum, where everything is of course in Spanish. Thus since my return, I have been translating every detail that I photographed along with the Argentine 1982/3 Rattenbach military report that was uncovered from the translation work because I found a copy on an Argentine government website.

The journey has been frustrating at times; especially the wait between the museum visit and the translation efforts, I don't speak

Spanish which only left machine translation, but it turned out to be readable. Now you can visit with me and understand better why the Falklands War came about. I know that we were ill-prepared to fight this war so far from home and acknowledge we had problems, but it was our efforts that won it.

The work of our military forces and supports organisations were the key to our success. Not just the organisations down South who were fantastic but also those at home and in this I include many businesses as well. We were professional, willing to learn and adapt, but what about our opponents, were they up to the job, could they have stopped us, should they even have been on the islands? Since the war much has been written about the Argentine performance but all that I have seen comes from our side, some of it praising them some not, in this book is both the Argentine view of Sovereignty and their view of their efforts in the war.

There are also pictures and translations of the Argentinian 1982 memorials, and each of them is different, the big city of Buenos Aires, the wildlife-rich Puerto Madryn and the almost threatening atmosphere of Ushuaia which was where the team from the car show "Top Gear" were attacked for having number plates that appeared to have some relevance to 1982.

The only victory I can claim in this book is that I did not have to write the Argentinian Spanish word for the Islands because it translates to "Falklands" which is lucky for me. After all, I just did not want to write it simply because the islands are The Falklands to me and always will be.

A lucky meeting

In Rio de Janeiro, Simon Weston (pictured with Cruise Director Neil Kelly) joined us as a Guest Speaker. Of course, I attended all of his events and his performance as a Speaker was second to none, I even managed a few words with him.

During a question and answer session, I was lucky enough to be able to ask if he had any advice for a veteran visiting Argentina. He was leaving the ship in Buenos Aires and had been there before to meet the man responsible for the attack on the Sir Galahad. His reply was simple and came from a Fawlty Towers classic "don't mention the war" which made complete sense and that was when I decided to go undercover. I had a good detailed map available on my tablet and surely as a military man, it would be possible to sneak in and out, or so I hoped.

Arrival in Buenos Aires

Initial investigations established the museum location is about 7 miles out of town which was well outside my walking capability, and that left buses, taxis and trains. The bus system was pronounced far too difficult by the tour office and a taxi would have meant talking to a local driver in English and he would, of course, know my destination, that would be the last option.

That left the train as my initial transport target, strangely the Argentine Railway system was mostly run by British companies in its early days. Locally they think we did not do a good job and there has been much discontent about our involvement. Let's face it, those railway companies were sold to us by Argentinian politicians: we did not force them to sell surely. I smell corruption which is probably endemic here if the rumours are true and the most significant factor in what is an almost failing country.

Finding enough time for my visit was going to be my biggest problem although we were staying overnight day 2 was fully committed to a ranch visit and Cunard was entertaining us from 2 pm on the 1st day, free drinks and a show could not be missed. To make matters worse, there was a shuttle to the terminal and another one into town; it all takes time, plus local security to get through in the terminal.

The only person aware of my plans was my wife and she had no wish to come with me (she probably thought I was mad). Disembarkation was then delayed by the non-arrival of the port authorities, did they know my intentions or was this normal here. The passengers' nationality on the ship was quite International although 60% were British. Half an hour later than hoped I managed to get onto the first shuttle, sailed through security and then sitting in the shuttle to town we went past the main railway station and on to the shuttle pick up point.

Walking the short distance to the station also took me past their 1982 memorial where there were few people around, but there were 2 soldiers already in place mounting a guard which was quite a good touch. The memorial seemed to be in a pleasant park area and was very well done, quite fitting. I took a few moments to pay my respects to the fallen and take a photograph; there are lots of names because they lost so many.

As I approached the railway station, there were more people around, and then I walked into this stunning architectural edifice.

The station building is in the Edwardian style and was British designed by Eustace L. Conder, Roger Conder and Sydney G. Follet together with an engineer Reginald Reynolds. Another example of our failings in running their railway, I think not as this would have been quite costly to build.

I had already established that the nearest station to my destination was called Nunez, and luckily all the trains to that station departed from the platform far left, this was a result, but now I needed a ticket. The booth is on the right and the young lady selling tickets had difficulty in recognising where I wanted to go. Showing the name on my map solved that problem; it's called "Nooness", of course. Then I tried to pay for my ticket, US dollars, "No", Credit Card, "No", only Argentinian cash would do for the $74 return fare, another problem.

Knowing that the Argentine Peso is in free fall meant we had not bought any before leaving the UK so I set off to get some change. Were they still trying to stop me getting to my destination or was I being paranoid but now I needed to find a bank or money changer. In Brazil ID was required to get cash and I had left my Passport in the cabin safe for safety reasons. Was this part of another plan to thwart my endeavours, I hoped not? Buenos Aires is like any large city, perhaps a bit cleaner than some but the pavements are littered with rough sleepers like most cities worldwide.

I start to wonder whether it would be better to get a taxi when I stumbled across one of those small money exchange offices with 3 little cubicles. In the booth, I handed over $10 US plus a few Brazil Reals I had remaining from our visit to Brazil and received $1400 pesos, a wallet full. My return train fare was, therefore, less than US 1$ and this confirms just how bad their economy is. I also breathed another sigh of relief as well because no ID was needed.

Back to the station again, and this is the 3rd time past the memorial which by this time is manned by 2 Argentinian sailors, nice to see, plus there were now a few tourist groups here. They are all being quiet and respectful; which is how it should be.

Luckily the ticket office window has no queue and is still being manned by the nice young girl I had spoken to earlier, she even recognised me, held up the same piece of paper with the price on and I gleefully handed over $100 in exchange for my passport to my destination which was just a piece of printed paper. The ticket barriers are all automated booths just like our underground, no use with my ticket and then I spotted a small manned gate. Showing my ticket, I was let in and then headed to the correct platform where the train was waiting.

The train was reasonably quiet, most people were heading into town at this time of day and I was going out. Plenty of seats to sit on in the carriage, it was clean, smart and left on time. When I got off in Nunez I was able to establish that there was a 12-minute service, which was brilliant for my return journey as time was passing far too quickly.

It was roughly 1 mile now to walk through a pleasant suburb and the weather was superb. As I marched onwards I contemplated what identity would be best for my visit if I did need to speak, French was my choice because I can get by in that language although my accent would be a giveaway, just speaking through my nose would probably solve that.

The complex finally came into view with many large brick-built buildings inside high iron railings, the main entrance was to the left up the main road but my map suggested a side entrance and I chose that one because it was quieter. At this gate, the guard did look at me questioningly but the mention of "Museo" brought a smile and the wave of a hand in the direction I was going anyway. Strangely many of the buildings had large black and white pictures of faces on them and they looked menacing or at least strange.

Later I found out that the museum is located in the International Centre for the Advancement of Human Rights in Buenos Aires, Argentina, and was established under the auspices of UNESCO, in Feb 2009, another troubling fact.

The origins of this site are worth studying, it was originally called ESMA which stands for Escuela Superior de Mecánica de la Armada, in other words, the Higher School of Mechanics of the Argentine Navy.

OK so far, we have something similar in our navy but it was here in ESMA from 1976 to 1983 that the buildings were used for the National Reorganization Process (Dirty War). Anyone who was opposed to the Junta or was thought to oppose them was tortured here, many were executed and female inmates even had babies conceived in the prison. After birth, the children were taken away and sold plus it is unlikely the mother survived. In Argentina these poor souls are known as the "Desaparecidos" or Disappeared, 30,000 in all. What went on here does not bear thinking about and I am glad I did not know these facts during my visit.

Since March 2004 the Argentine government has established this as a dedicated place of remembrance, protection and human rights defence on the premises of the ESMA, which explains all the pictures I had seen on the buildings and the last thing I wanted to do was become a member of the "Desaparecidos".

Of course, UNESCO would support this as they try to establish human rights worldwide; there are many countries where human rights are non-existent. The museum was opened in 2012 and I wonder if they know about it, UNESCO stands for United Nations Educational Scientific and Cultural Organisation. Education should be balanced so that each of us can make our judgements and thus be better members of the human race.

The Museum at last and the Belgrano

Finally, I breathed a sigh of relief as I reached my target, but it looked closed, even deserted although it should have been open according to the web. The museum sign on the low wall had distracted me and as I skirted around the building I missed the main entrance which was just over my right shoulder in this photograph.

The FALKLANDS MUSEUM AND ISLANDS OF THE SOUTH ATLANTIC is the translation, and not wanting to waste my efforts I circled the building to at least study the exterior.

No one was about at all, and at the other side of this large building is a hefty pond with a concrete copy of the islands in the middle. On the far side of it is a memorial to the Belgrano made up of a rusty sheet steel outlines of the ship along with detailed plaques.

Every exhibit in the museum is naturally written in Spanish and I have used Google translate to create an English version, changing the translation slightly to make it read better without, I hope, altering the intended meaning. Where I comment on the text I have put in bold italic brackets my thoughts and opinions, (***This is the time to state that I support the Falkland Islanders rights first and last but also hope that Argentina finds a way to move forward.***)

The exhibit text is on panels sunk below the level of the pond on the far side of the building in a location that would approximate to where she was sunk, this makes sense. The picture of the exhibit and pond was taken from the upper floor of the museum, it was open after all and so my journey would not be wasted. From an aerial perspective, the building and grounds appear to represent a map view of Argentina.

HISTORY OF THE ARA GENERAL BELGRANO

The Cruiser, of American origin, was built on March 12, 1938, and named USS Phoenix. As part of the fleet that participated in World War II, she survived the Japanese attack on Pearl Harbour that started the Pacific War in 1941.

In 1943, she transported the North American Secretary of State, Cordell Hull, to Morocco, when Churchill and Roosevelt made an Anglo-North American alliance to demand the surrender of the Axis forces.

In December of that year, USS Phoenix joined the U.S. Navy's Seventh Fleet and took the first offensive action on the island of New Britain, northern Australia.

On several of its missions in the Pacific, the Phoenix was accompanied by its twin Boise. Both were bought by Argentina in 1951, under the presidency of General Juan Domingo Perón.

Thus, on April 12, 1951, flying the Argentine flag, they are renamed, the USS Phoenix: ARA "October 17" and the USS Boise: ARA "July 9" at the Philadelphia Naval Base.

During the coup d'état against Perónism in 1955, the Cruiser would play a significant role and be later renamed with its final name.

During the following years, she continued with her varied activity, fulfilling search and rescue tasks, logistic ship, troop transport, dissuasion, surface operations, amphibious operations, artillery training, professional training, as a missile school, sea patrol, training of applicants, cadet training ship, among others.

On February 12, 1982, she went to Puerto Belgrano for the maintenance that the Cruiser needed each year. But on April 2 the entire crew was enlisted in a war mission, a complement of 1091 sailors and 2 civilians. She set sail on April 16 as part of Task Force 79.3.

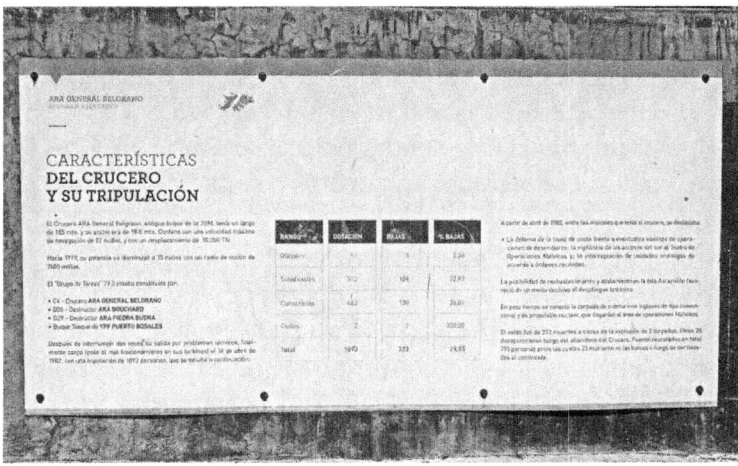

DETAILS OF THE CRUISER AND ITS CREW

• The ARA General Belgrano Cruiser, a former 2GM vessel, had a length of 185 meters, and its width was 18.8 meters. It had a maximum speed of 22 knots and a displacement of 10,000 TN.

By 1979, its speed was reduced to 15 knots with a radius of 7600 miles of action.

The -Task Force- 79.3 consisted of
• CL, - ARA GENERAL BELGRANO Cruiser
• D26 - ARA BOUCHARD Destroyer
• D29 - ARA PIEDRA BUENA Destroyer
• YPF LIGHT TANK Ship

AFTER two interruptions to its departure for technical problems, finally sailed (despite malfunction in its turbines) on April 16, 1982, with a crew of 1093 people, detailed below:

STATUS	NUMBERS	DEAD	% DEAD
Officers	56	3	5.36
Regulars	572	188	32.87
Conscripts	463	130	28.08
Civilians	2	2	100
Total	1093	323	29.95

(Note: seeing 2 civilians on the list is quite a surprise, I am unable to establish what they were doing on board but would imagine they were engineers given the turbine problems.)

From April 1982, among the missions of the cruiser, was highlighted:

• The defence of the coastline against possible attempts at landing operations; surveillance of southern access to the Falklands Operations Theatre and; interception of enemy units. According to orders received.

The possibility of disrupting resupply and use of The Ascension Island decisively thus stopping the British deployment.

It was known that in a short time there would be the departure of English submarines of the conventional type and nuclear propulsion, which would reach the Falklands area of operations.

There were 272 deaths from the explosion of 2 torpedoes.

Another 28 disappeared after the cruiser sank.

A total of 793 people were rescued, including 23 that died on the life rafts or after being airlifted to the mainland.

ATTACK and SINKING
OF CRUISER
ARA GENERAL BELGRANO.

16:01. A powerful stern explosion violently shook the ship paralyzing its 1093 crew members, followed by the immediate cessation of power and all lighting.

Four decks were holed and there were 270 casualties. Quickly there was a second explosion from another torpedo of equal magnitude, destroying the bow, generating two new deaths.

Two torpedoes 6.5 m long, 0.5 m in diameter and 1.5 t of total weight (365 kg of explosive each), launched by the nuclear submarine HMS Conqueror, and had fulfilled their task.

16:08. They were rushing onto the ship's outer deck, receiving orders through hand megaphones and being broadcast by shouting. Crew members carried wounded comrades on their shoulders, there was fire, floods, darkness and calls for help were over-heard.

16:10. Inclination was increasing by 1 degree per minute. The hull was sinking with a higher prevalence to the stern, due to a large amount of water in the hangar and the engine room. The ship had 72 life rafts. The rafts were thrown into the water, which opened automatically when they floated.

16:18. A 20-degree tilt and the oil on the deck made it difficult to walk. It was necessary to hold on to the structure of the ship or ropes, so as not to slip or fall into the sea.

The hull continued to penetrate the water so that the main deck on the ship was already flush with the waves. The situation tended to worsen and this was the point of no return. All that was missing was the order of the command to leave the ship.

16:23. After a tense wait, there was no longer any possible alternative: the commander ordered everyone to abandon ship. The wounded were the first transhipped to the rafts, in a delicate manoeuvre. After that, vision and communication between the rafts have become impossible.

It was feared that the submerged stern and hull would form a void, and drag the nearest rafts to the bottom of the sea.

16.50. The 60-degree inclination was the start of the sinking. An intense smoke was coming from inside, increasing the drama of the moment. It was known that no one was left alive outside the rafts.

17:00. The sinking.

Long live the Fatherland! Long live the Belgrano! Were the cries heard from the rafts; watching the total and final sinking of the ARA General Belgrano as thousands of tons of water managed to cover her?

(For any mariner this was a tragic event that unfortunately had to take place, it was significant in the war for many reasons and I found this part a bit difficult just because I can imagine the event from a fellow sailor's point of view.

The Belgrano is now a war grave as is the other ships that were sunk, some of my shipmates rest in the Sheffield and Coventry, may they all Rest in Peace.

I did expect to find the translated words point the finger of blame but that is not here, just facts and figures that bring the realism of war and things that happen.

Looking at the casualty figures are revealing, only 3 officers died, and these would probably have been engineers on watch down below.

Any navy that has conscription is run mostly by the regulars and that would explain why they are the majority that died.

I do not favour conscription; the great majority of our forces were regulars and this contributed a great deal to our success.)

21

Museum Layout

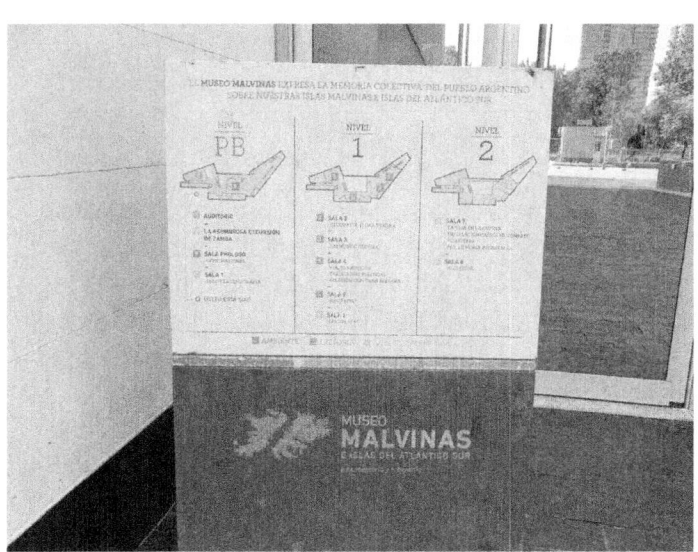

We are about to enter what is quite an imposing building, I was impressed with the outside, this museum is considerably larger than the one in Stanley but of course, it's the displays and artefacts that are important.

THE FALKLANDS MUSEUM EXPRESSES THE COLLECTIVE MEMORY OF THE ARGENTINIAN PEOPLE ON OUR FALKLANDS ISLANDS AND ISLANDS OF THE SOUTH ATLANTIC

	LEVEL GF		LEVEL 1		LEVEL 2
A	AUDITORIUM	2	ROOM 2	7	ROOM 7
Z	ZAMBA's AMAZING EXCURSION.		GEOGRAPHY, FLORA AND FAUNA		LIFE IN WAR INSTALLATION FALLS IN COMBAT POSTWAR PERIOD PEACE, MEMORY AND SOVEREIGNTY
P	INTRODUCTION ROOM	3	ROOM 3	8	ROOM 8
	FALKLANDS TIMELINE		RAYMUNDO GLEYZER		MEDIA SECTION
1	ROOM 1	4	ROOM 4		
	TEMPORARY EXHIBIT		NAUTICAL TRIPS POLITICAL TRADITIONS RELATIONSHIP WITH GREAT BRITAIN		
*	YOU ARE HERE	5	ROOM 5		
			BIOGRAPHIES		
		6	ROOM 6		
			THE 3 PLAZAS		

The Auditorium is where visitors are greeted, there is a small central reception desk manned by a lady and there were at least 3 people in what looked like a cloakroom. There were several other attendants dotted about and no visitors around apart from me.

Therefore quite a few members of staff and no entrance fee, quite an expensive operation and there was not even the normal café that you see in most museums. Someone is paying for this operation.

The building inside is very open, plenty of glass which let in lots of light and the upper floors have open sections in them to provide space for a light aeroplane that is hanging from the roof.

ZAMBA's AMAZING EXCURSION (Z)

Immediately to the left is this large area set aside for visiting school children.

There is an enormous board on the wall that is filled with drawings done by them. At the top is a cartoon which says "enough censor" (basta de censu) and I suspect is supposed to encourage them to write whatever they want.

Seeing this space lifted my hopes, it is an indication that "The Argentinian view on Sovereignty of the Falkland" is part of every child's education but it is not the proof that I wanted.

What I wanted to know was, what are they being told, and when did it all start? It is only indoctrination of the people of Argentina that can instil in them the views that we see being expressed so often in public.

Initially, I thought ZAMBA was a reference to a traditional Argentine folk dance which is a little like a rumba but is different in musicality, rhythm, and temperament. It is a majestic dance with 6 beats to the bar and is performed by couples waving handkerchiefs and circling each other. We were to see many performances by couples in traditional costume, stepping elegantly around each other, almost as if they are trying to attract each other in a courtship routine.

Now I can reveal that ZAMBA is a cartoon character from an Argentine state-run TV channel Paka Paka. In the Falklands visit episode shown in 2012 (which can be seen on U-tube) he time travels to the islands in 1982 and meets military from both sides and locals. The characterisation is as expected nationalistic and reinforces in children's minds the Argentine claim to the islands.

The pictures in the next chapter (Falklands Timeline) are of a large circular display with a timeline running around the bottom half, and for this, there are translations for each year.

The top half of the exhibit provides information about periods of history with some relevant pictures/graphics and headings. These I have identified with numbers, 1, 2, etc. and you can then refer to these numbers in my translations.

FALKLANDS TIMELINE (P)

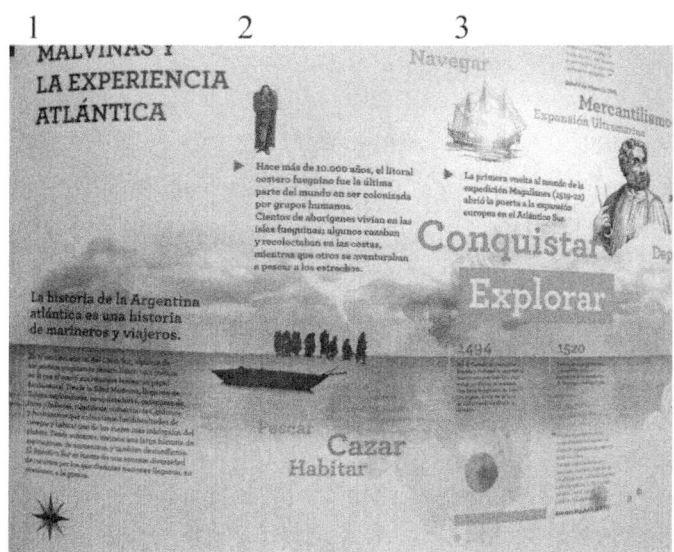

FALKLANDS THE ATLANTIC EXPERIENCE

Fishing
Hunt
Live

1 The history of Atlantic Argentina is a history of sailors and travellers. At the southern end of the Southern Cone, some of the native peoples developed a culture in which the sea and its resources played a key role. From the Modern Age, explorers, conquerors, seal and whale hunters, scientists, traders, settlers and officials have arrived from Europe and faced the difficulties of navigating and inhabiting one of the most inhospitable seas on the planet. Since then, we have lived a long history of aspirations, of encounters, and also of conflicts. The

South Atlantic is the source of a huge diversity of resources for which different nations sometimes came to war.

2 More than 10,000 years ago, the Fuegian *(an Indian people of Tierra del Fuego)* coastal coastline was the last part of the world to be colonized by human groups. Hundreds of Aboriginal people lived on the Fuegian islands; some hunted and collected on the shores, while others ventured to fish in the straits.

3 The first round-the-world tour of the Magellan expedition (1519-22) opened the door to European expansion in the South Atlantic.

Conquer
To explore

1494
By the Treaty of Tordesillas, Spain and Portugal divide the world yet to be discovered to avoid conflicts of interest.
An imaginary line - the "stripe" - 370 leagues east of the Cape Verde Islands, established the division.
(Britain was not involved in this Treaty and therefore is not subject to the clauses, and has no relevance to a Sovereignty claim by Argentina.)

1520
Possible Falklands sighting by deserting sailors from the Hernando de Magallanes expedition.
"One day, when we least expected it, a gigantic-looking man appeared before us.
He was on the sand almost naked, singing and dancing at the same time, dusting himself on his head [...]The captain-general called these towns 'Patagones'."
Antonio Pigafetta (s, XVI)
(Most historians believe the giants here are almost certainly Tehuelche Indians living on the mainland, not the Falklands.)

Plunder

1   "We had all day strong storms, rough sea and very hectic, with stormy and incredibly large waves. We had wet and windy weather with lots of snow and hail."
Willem Schouten (s.XVI)

2   The South Atlantic provided Europeans with natural resources such as skins and fat from marine animals in the area.

3   "No animal to fear for its ferocity, its poison or its siege, an innumerable number of the most useful amphibians, highly exquisite birds and fish, combustible material to fill the shortage of wood, plants that served for the diseases of the navigators."
Louis Antoine de Bougainville (s.XVIII)

4   From the Enlightenment, European "scientific" travellers came to the South Atlantic eager to measure and classify life in the area without considering those who preceded them.

1600

Dutchman Sebald de Weert spots an archipelago belonging to the Falklands.

(There is no reference on the timeline of John Davis and the Desire visit of 1592.

What about John Strong's visit in 1690 when he named the passage between the islands Falkland Channel?

Now I start to see how Argentina is conveniently leaving out facts to manipulate the people. It is called indoctrination.)

(This text below relates to the picture of a seal being killed.)
His official report regarding the Island of South Georgia, in which he tells about a large number of sea elephants and sea lions.
James Weddell (1825)

To seize
Sort out
Describe

1767

French crown recognizes Spanish sovereignty over the Falkland Islands and handed over the colony founded by Louis Antoine Bougainville in 1764 to the Spanish authorities of Buenos Aires. Port Louis is renamed Puerto Soledad.

(In 1765 Port Egmont was discovered by John Byron and colonised in 1766.

In 1770 the Spanish expelled the British by force after shots were fired. The British complained and in 1771 a Declaration was signed that restored the situation on the Falklands to the condition in 1770, in other words, the Spanish backed down.)

1774

The English evacuate Port Egmont, founded clandestinely in 1766, and recognize Spanish sovereignty.

(When the British decided to stop manning Port Egmont a plaque was left to proclaim British sovereignty. Britain did NOT recognise the Spanish claim; Queen Elizabeth 1 rejected it, the first untruth.)

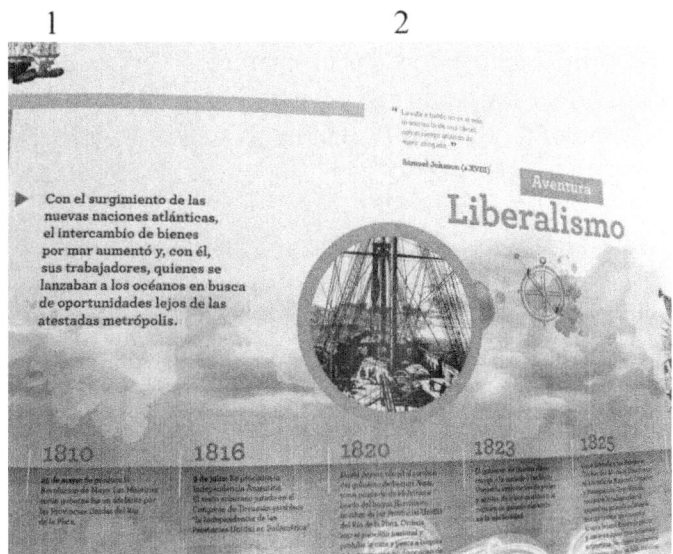

1   With the emergence of the new Atlantic nations, the exchange of goods by sea increased and, with it, its workers, who launched themselves into the oceans in search of opportunities far from the crowded metropolises.

2   "Life on board is no more or less that of a prison, with the added risk of drowning."
Samuel Johnson (18th century)

Adventure
Liberalism

1810
May 25: May Revolution occurs. The Falklands will henceforth be ruled by the United Provinces of the Río de la Plata.

(This was a revolution, not a transfer of power by Spain and they evacuated Port Louis in 1811. There is no evidence that The Falklands would be ruled by the United Provinces.)

1816
July 9: Argentine Independence is proclaimed.
The sovereign text sworn in the Congress of Tucumán establishes "the Independence of the United Provinces in South America".

1820
David Jewett, an officer in the service of the government of Buenos Aires, takes possession of Falklands aboard the ship Heroine on behalf of the United Provinces of the Río de la Plata. Orders the hoisting of the national flag and prohibits hunting and fishing of foreign vessels that do not have permission.

(The American privateer Jewett spent only 6 months at Port Louis and was assisted by the British Explorer James Weddell. Jewett escaped to Brazil in 1822 when accused of piracy by a Portuguese court. The majority of people living in Port Louis at the time were British and American.)

1823
The government grants the Pacheco-Vernet society the exploitation of skins and oils of sea lions and the capture of wild cattle on East Falkland.
(They had to get permission from the British Ambassador.)

1825
Great Britain, the United Provinces of the Rio de la Plata founded the Treaty of Friendship, Trade and Navigation: Britain recognizes Argentine independence, agrees to immigration and investment policies and accepts the ban on fishing and hunting in Argentine jurisdictional waters. Do not object to Argentina's sovereignty over the Falkland Islands.

(The Falkland Islands was not mentioned in the document at all; surely if Argentina had wanted they could have mentioned the

islands instead of later claiming that we did not object, I do not think an agreement of omission has any standing in law.)

People settled

1   In the early 19th century, the Falkland Islands became a strategic location. The River Plate government took steps to control the area. This caused an American attack in 1831 and another in 1833 by the British who took the colony and occupied the Islands ever since.

(The British have governed the islands continuously apart from the short period in 1982 when Argentina invaded until they were thrown out. Argentinians have always been welcomed as settlers but very few came, life on these remote islands requires a certain type of person who is prepared for the conditions.)

Hides/skins

1828

The Governor of Buenos Aires, Manuel Dorrego grants several leagues of land to Luis Vernet in Falklands in exchange for founding a colony there within three years. Vernet orders the shipment to the islands of thirty blacks with their respective families, horses and various supplies. A year later he was appointed civil and military - commandant' of the islands.

"1 Monday 20 July 1829

Same weather and wind, I moved into my new room today; this one has two large windows that look at the bay where the ships enter. The piano was landed, the one that arrived without any harm, everyone danced except me that I barely have a face to play the piano wrong. "

Maria Vernet

1830

She was born in the Islands Matilde Malvina Vernet, the daughter of Luis Vernet and María Sáez. She is the first Argentine recognized in our Falklands.

1831

The American warship Lexington ravages Port Louis in retaliation for the capture, under Vernet's orders, of many ships of that nationality that stole our wildlife. The crew members of the American ship looted houses and ranches, and apprehend many Argentinians who inhabited the Falklands. Argentina protests immediately. The schooner Sarandí transports the new authorities to restore the order broken by the Lexington attack.

1833

January 3: Troops of Great Britain aboard the Corvette Clio occupy and usurp the Falklands.

Colonel Pinedo returns to Buenos Aires without a battle. Gauchos and other settlers remain in the Islands of their own free will. The attack has happened in times of peace between the two nations. Argentina immediately protests against Britain's policy of colonial expansion.

August 26: Incidents between the British occupiers and the Gauchos of Antonio Rivero.

The social causes of the uprising, the payment on worthless paper vouchers and labour abuse add to the feeling of pride of the gauchos' sense of sovereignty.

(The majority of Colonel Pinedo's troops were actually British and they were unwilling to fight their own countrymen.

Antonio Rivero was not the hero portrayed here, he murdered 5 leading members of the Port Louis community including Vernet's Deputy Mathew Brisbane, and there is Argentinian documentation that verifies this. The remaining residents fled and the Gauchos remained in control.)

"It was very surprising to see the gauchos light fire immediately, with nothing but tinder and a piece of cloth in the rain and all soaked."
Charles Darwin (s.XIX)

1834

The Beagle, FitzRoy's ship, at the Falklands. Scientist Charles Darwin travels on board. It is one of the most important scientific trips in the history of the world embarking the rebel gauchos who had starred in incidents the previous year.

(The Beagle did call in on her 2nd voyage and helped to put down the revolt, returning them in chains to either Britain or Argentina. The British encouraged the remaining Argentinian settlers to stay on the islands.)

1841

England colonizes the Falklands and appoints the first British governor: Richard Clement Moody. It creates Port Stanley, where twelve English sappers are to live with their families. The Argentine Confederation protests again against the occupation.

(This period in the Falkland Island history is where the Sovereignty question is somewhat blurred especially with the documentation.

The Argentine case is based on the fact that the agreement in 1825 contains no reference to the islands.

The facts are however that the Argentine people have never been happy to live in this place; even in 1825, it was mostly British who lived and worked in what was then quite an inhospitable place.

Their efforts to colonise were inept and badly managed so that in 1833 it was the British who successfully colonised from that time till now.)

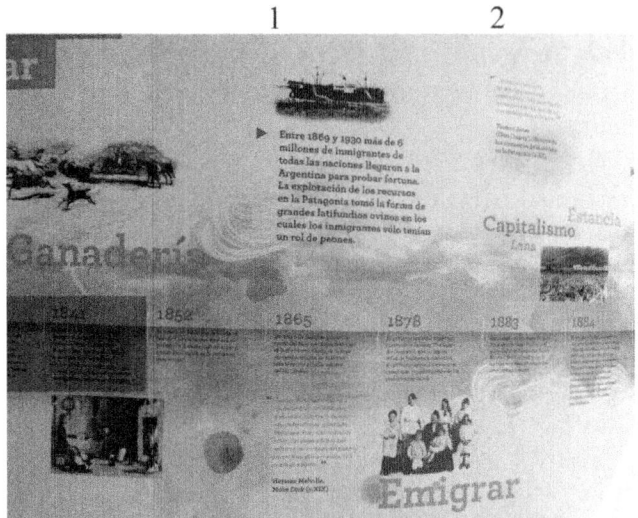

Cattle raising

1   Between 1869 and 1930 more than 6 million immigrants from all nations came to Argentina to make their fortune. The exploitation of resources in Patagonia took the form of large sheep estates in which immigrants had only a peasant role.

2   "... we were soon accused of worries and adversities. After landing in a wasteland, far from the comforts of civilization."
Thomas Jones
(Glan Camwy), History of the beginnings of the colony in Patagonia (twentieth century)

Capitalism
Wool
South American Farm

1852
The Falkland Islands Company is installed in the Falklands, which will exercise a monopoly for almost a century and a half. It is the beginning of the wool-sheep industry.
(It was the Argentinian hero Vernet who sold the rights to the founder of the Company, British merchant G T Whittington.)

1865
A group of Welsh families, aboard the Mimosa, lands in the New Gulf. As water was scarce in the area, they settle further south, in the lower valley of the Chubut River.
"Although the world disdains the whalers, however, and without being aware of it, they pay us the ignited tribute. For almost all the candles, lamps and spark plugs that burn in the far reaches of the globe do so, for our glory, with whale oil."
Herman Melville,
Moby Dick (s.XIX)
(The southern part of Argentina was finally settled by Welsh people; again the locals were not prepared to put up with the hardship of living in less welcoming places.)

1878
The Argentine national government begins the so-called "Conquest of the Desert", which incorporates thousands of square kilometres into the national territory by extermination and confinement of the native peoples.
(This is another example of oppression in this country. If Britain were to do it would be called Imperialism.)

Emigration

1883
Stimulated by the travels of Luis Piedrabuena, the governor of Santa Cruz, Carlos Moyano visits Falklands. Sheep are traded between the mainland and the Islands and settlers are exchanged.

1884
Argentine Navy Colonel Augusto Lasserre founded the city of Ushuaia in the Grande Tierra del Fuego Island. There was a religious mission whose head, Thomas Bridges, raised the British flag and the Argentine one in recognition of sovereignty.

Argentina demands an international arbitration to settle the conflict with Britain over the Falklands.
(One of many claims over the years.)

1   The Industrial Revolution increased the demand for whale fat in Europe, taking its hunting to levels never seen before. With the invention of the harpoon gun in the early twentieth century, there was the almost total predation of cetaceans.

2   "During a particularly calm night, we were surprised several times by the strong blowing of the whales between us and the coast."
Philip Parker King (s.XIX)

Imperialism
2nd Industrial Revolution.
Extinction

1902
With the signing of the "Pactos of May", the possibilities of war for border issues with Chile are ended.

1904
The Argentine government establishes the magnetic and meteorological observatory of Laurie Island, in the South Orkney Islands. It is the first permanent settlement in Antarctica on February 22, 1904, the Argentine flag is planted on the island; Today is Antarctica Day.
(It has long been my opinion that Argentina was looking to establish her rights to Antarctica and its huge resources in wildlife and minerals. If you look at any map, without the Falklands and other islands, they have no claim at all.)

Argentina starts the activities of the Argentine Fishing Company, an important whaling establishment in the Port of Grytviken, in the South Georgia Islands.
(The company was started by 3 foreign nationals who resided in Buenos Aires, the Norwegian consul P. Christophersen, H.H. Schlieper (US national), and E. Tornquist (a Swedish banker). It was the idea of the explorer Carl A Larsen and he managed the business, so it was Argentinian only in name. The lease was granted by the Governor of the Falkland Island.)

"And yet I would like to go through those sensations again. For several years I would like to return to the icy regions. I would like to hear again in that silence of death the noise of the blizzard, the whistling of wind and snow on the flanks of the tent."
José María Sobral (s.XX).

1910

Paul Groussac defends the Argentine rights over the Falklands through historical and legal arguments that support the Argentine Republic to claim them. He does so in his work Les Iles Malouines (The Falkland Islands), written in French.

1914

There is a naval battle between a fleet of the German Imperial Navy and the British in waters outside the Falklands, during World War I. The archipelago remains a strategic place.

Resources and Strategies

1 Argentine state-owned enterprises played a central role in The Patagonian Population. This model of development and industrialization, sustained by ups and downs for decades, was hit hard in the mid-1970s and abandoned in the mid-1990s.

1920

A group of South Georgian workers organizes a strike and sets out among its goals the organization of all whaling workers in the world.

They are repressed and deported to the mainland by British sailors. Meanwhile, in Santa Cruz, strikes by Patagonian rural peasants are bloodied by the Argentine national government in defence of the interests of the great landowners.

Oil is of fundamental and irreplaceable importance, and the nation's growth and progress will be all the greater with the firm control of its oilfields."

Enrique Mosconi (s.XX)

1934

Alfredo Palacios, Socialist MP, succeeds in getting the Congress to approve the translation into Spanish of Groussac's book, Les Iles Malouines (The Falkland Islands), and that it is used in the training of future teachers.

(Once the teachers are trained then the subject can be included in the children's curriculum. The book they use is a shortened version of Groussac's original and I will never find a copy, however, this museum is slowly revealing the facts as seen by Argentina, some lies and plenty of missing historical facts. At least I now know who started it and when.)

1937

Protest of the Youth Radical Orientation Force.

Argentina (FORJA) (e Young Argentina) for the erection of a statue to George Canning, a symbol of British colonialism. The Falklands are consolidated as a symbol of the subjugation relationship with that power.

(George Canning was the British Foreign Secretary from 1822 to 1827 and granted recognition to Argentina, thus freeing them from the yoke of Colonial Spain. Argentina wanted independence but now had to contend with the commercial aspects of the world. From now on the Government of Argentina would start its downward spiral into corruption, something that they blame the British for; it's never their fault it seems.)

1   Since the beginning of the 20th century, many nations of the world have set out to explore and occupy the Southern Cone. Argentina has played a permanent and sustained role in this task since 1904, making it one of the countries with the greatest presence and Antarctic history.

1941
Falklands in the school curriculum: the "Falklands question" becomes a mandatory subject of teaching in schools through disciplines such as Geography and History.
(Now they start to indoctrinate the children of Argentina with the "Falklands question" which is the Argentinian view of the history of the islands and that the islands belong to them.
This museum is a demonstration of that view and that is why they will always support the recovery of the islands. Essentially everyone over the age of 85 has now been indoctrinated. Unfortunately, there is only their side of the story being told, plus the politicians use this to distract attention when it suits them.
The museum is based in a complex which is supposed to be dedicated to reconciliation but this cannot occur whilst this

education policy is in place. If they wanted to solve the problem they should introduce both sides of the argument, in time the people will understand and then there can be reconciliation.)

1942
An Argentine ship, on May 1, sails for Deception Island, to take formal possession of the Argentine Antarctic Sector.

"The Argentine Republic has almost four thousand kilometres of river and maritime coast, but, because of the convenience of the railway, the Republic, from the point of view of international trade, was a considered a Mediterranean country."

(This seems to be a complaint that the railway is holding them back from developing their own shipping.)

1946
The Argentine government presents to the first General Assembly of the United Nations its reservation of sovereignty rights over The Falkland Islands.

1951
A first scientific expedition to the Argentine Antarctic, under the command of Colonel Pujato. On March 21, the General San Martin base was inaugurated, the first Argentine settlement south of the Antarctic polar circle, which constitutes it as the southernmost base in the world.

1959
ANTARCTIC TREATY: It is the legal-political instrument regulating Antarctic activities, signed on 1 December 1959 by the principal countries during the International Geophysical Year (AGI). On 25 April 1961, it was effectively sanctioned as a Law of Nation No. 15.802.

1960
The UN adopts resolution 1514, which proclaims the need to end colonialism. Falklands is one of the cases to be solved.

Diplomacy

1964
Civilian aviator Miguel Fitzgerald lands in the Falklands aboard his small Cessna 185 aircraft. Flies the Argentine flag and delivers a proclamation in favour of the sovereignty claim. A crowd receives him when he returns to the mainland.
(This plane is hanging from the ceiling in the middle of the museum; I took a picture of it when on the top floor.)

1965
FIRST EXPEDITION BY ARGENTINA TO THE SOUTH POLE:
Colonel Jorge E. Leal and nine men from the Argentine Army arrive at the Geographical South Pole.

1966
Operation Condor. Seven Argentine flags fly in the Falklands. Led by Dardo Cabo, 18 young people – mostly identified with Perónism – hijack a plane from Aerolíneas Argentinas and land in the Falklands. They rename Port Stanley as "Puerto Rivero" and proclaim Argentine sovereignty.

1968

Argentina and Great Britain sign a Memorandum of Understanding. The English undertake to recognize Argentine sovereignty in the Islands based on respect for the interests of the islanders by Argentina.

(It is true that there was a draft document between the 2 governments but it was never signed so the above statement is a lie. The plan was leaked to the islanders by the Governor and pressure on the Conservative Party forced its withdrawal. Although this plan would have prevented the Falklands war Argentina would likely have changed the islander's way of life forever.)

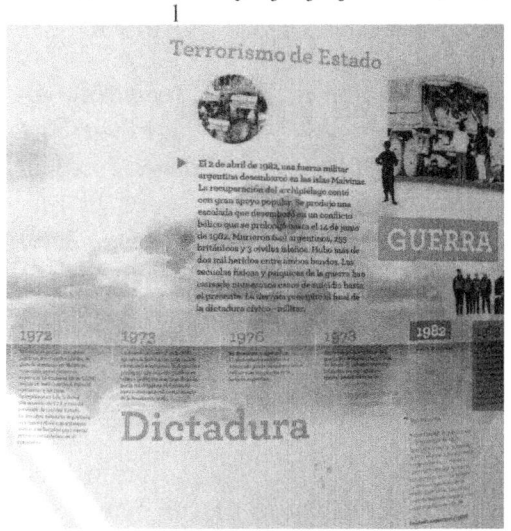

State terrorism

1 On 2 April 1982, an Argentine military force landed in the Falklands Islands. The recovery of the archipelago had great popular support. There was an escalation that led to a war that lasted until 14 June 1982. 649 Argentines, 255 Britons and 3 island civilians were killed. There were more than two thousand wounded between the two sides. The physical and psychosomatic aftermath of the war has caused numerous suicide cases to date. Defeat precipitated the end of the civic-military dictatorship.

(It is interesting for me to see that many of the Argentine militaries also suffered from mental health issues after the war as did many British servicemen and Islanders.)

1972

The Argentine state inaugurates, together with island authorities, the airstrip in The Falklands, built by the Argentine government. The air company LADE operates a weekly flight between the mainland and the Islands. A YPF station and a state gas supply station are established in East Falkland. In two years Argentine teachers teach in Falklands and young islanders have scholarships to study secondary school on the continent.

(Relationships between the UK and Argentina are good as the British Government pushes the islanders towards Argentina. The type 42 Destroyer ARA Hercules was ordered in 1970 and I was on HMS Sheffield in 1974 whilst she was built in the same Barrow shipyard, at times the two ships were berthed together.)

Dictatorship

1973

Assembly approves Resolution 3160, where it recognizes Argentina's efforts to achieve a peaceful solution around the dispute with Great Britain for sovereignty in the Falklands. Compliance with Resolution 2065 is again urged.

1976

March 24: Military strike. The democratic government is overthrown by the bloodiest civic-military dictatorship in Argentine history.

1978

Argentina and Chile on the brink of war over a dispute about the Beagle Channel. The Argentine government had ignored an unfavourable arbitration award in 1977.

WAR

1982
Falklands War

Guerra de Falklands
"Dear Mother:
On this piece of paper, I want to express to you all my love, gratitude and desires that together we will read this letter and that as we read it we will understand. (...) do not know whether I will be able to face death with dignity, as a man, or as you would like. I'm scared like everyone else, but I know I'm defending my homeland and I'm proud of it."
Old-Argentine (1982)
(The indoctrination at school is still in place but the rank and file know that things will not go well.)

War veteran
Globalization Former Combatant

Sustainable Exploitation

1983
On the first anniversary of the Falklands War, former fighters mobilize. They call for social recognition and denounce the growing process of forgetfulness and segregation. December 1983 is the end of the dictatorship. The people vote in October, regain democracy and Dr Raúl Alfonsín assumes the presidency.

1985
Inauguration of Mount Pleasant military base.

1989
Umbrellas of sovereignty to advance collaboration agreements and restore diplomatic relations between Argentina and the United Kingdom.
Weekly flights between Chile and The Falklands. Argentines can visit the islands again. Fishing agreement between Argentines and Britons, with island participation.

1994
The Falklands question assumes constitutional rank. The Argentine Nation ratifies its legitimate and imprescriptible sovereignty over the Falklands, South Georgia and South Sandwich areas and the corresponding maritime and island areas for being an integral part of the national territory. The recovery of those territories and the full exercise of sovereignty, respecting the way of life of its inhabitants and following the principles of international law, constitute a permanent and indispensable objective of the Argentine people.

2005
The Argentine government denounces the collaboration agreements on fishing and hydrocarbons for breaches by Great Britain.

1   They wanted us to eat from the crumbs of oblivion
But there are no pigeons left after a War.
Chicks of condor tearing the guts of the truth
Gustavo Caso Rosendi,
"In El Palomar"

Sovereignty
PEACE Memory

2009
UNASUR, Union of South American Nations, is speaking in Quito, Ecuador, for the defence of Argentine sovereignty on the Falklands issue.

2010
Announcement of the oil finds in the Falklands.

2011
The cause for The Argentine sovereignty of the Falklands receives historical support from all Latin American and Caribbean countries,

represented in CELAC, Community of Latin American and the Caribbean States.

2012

Official publication of the Rattenbach Report in Argentina. Request to the Red Cross to collaborate in the identification of the Argentine Military buried in the Falklands.

(The Rattenbach Report had been commissioned by the military junta in 1983. The publication allowed me to obtain a Spanish copy and translate it so that I could include some extracts and relevant comments in a later chapter.

Finally, Argentina decides to take some sensible action about their dead in the Falklands which hopefully will give some closure to their relatives.)

2014

The Falklands and South Atlantic Islands Museum open on the Day of affirmation of Argentine Rights on the Falklands, Islands and Antarctic Sector.

(This giant circular exhibit has been designed to dominate the ground floor and has provided me with a great deal of information.

I believe that the display can only represent the information being used in the schools.

It is a history of some lies, partial truths and missing facts designed to lead the viewer along the Argentinian path of righteousness.

Knowing that this education policy has been in place for so long is it any wonder that the public act and feel as they do.

Finally, I believe that I have the evidence to say that this is truly the INDOCTRINATION of a nation.

Argentina has been beset with many problems mostly because their politicians are corrupt, however, in this case, they have created a situation that is almost impossible to rectify.

Add to that the option to blame someone else, especially imperialism and those politicians always feel they can manipulate the public.

Although Argentina professes to be a Democracy, it is not because the Perónists, who are dictators, appear to hold the power and continue to rob the people.

Having established a position that the Falklands belong to Argentina, any government is left with no option but to continue with the rhetoric or the people will not support them, which is why they regularly bring the subject up.)

TEMPORARY EXHIBIT (1)

The final and second exhibit on the extremely large ground floor is almost hidden in a corner.

The title is MY PHOTO OF FALKLANDS.

In 2016 our museum launched a call for the public to share their photographs related to Falklands.

Images taken with non-professional cameras, showing how many people had chosen to portray themselves concerning the islands.

This exhibition is a selection of the material received and an invitation to continue sending us their photographs.

POSTWAR

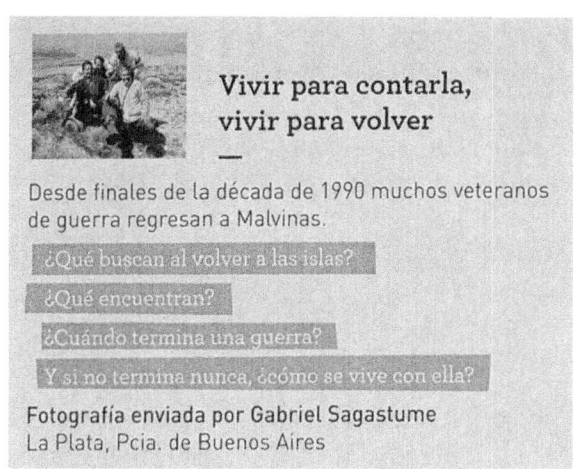

> **Vivir para contarla, vivir para volver**
>
> Desde finales de la década de 1990 muchos veteranos de guerra regresan a Malvinas.
>
> ¿Qué buscan al volver a las islas?
> ¿Qué encuentran?
> ¿Cuándo termina una guerra?
> Y si no termina nunca, ¿cómo se vive con ella?
>
> Fotografía enviada por Gabriel Sagastume
> La Plata, Pcia. de Buenos Aires

Living to tell it,
living to come back

From the late 1990s, many war veterans return to the Falklands.
What are you looking for when you return to the islands?
What do you find?
When does it end?
And if it never ends, how do you live with it?

(I am sure that many British veterans will relate to these comments, PTSD has no borders and no nationality, it lies in wait, striking at any time when you are least expecting it.)

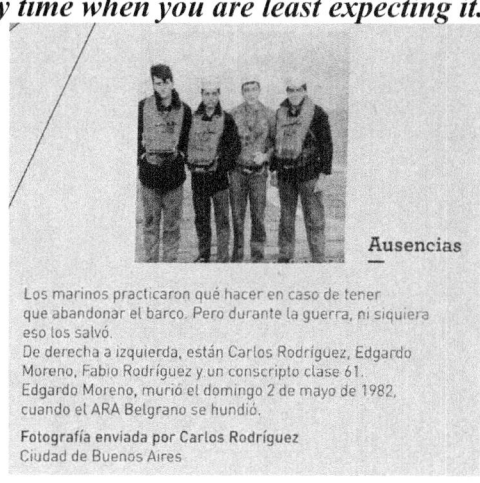

> **Ausencias**
>
> Los marinos practicaron qué hacer en caso de tener que abandonar el barco. Pero durante la guerra, ni siquiera eso los salvó.
> De derecha a izquierda, están Carlos Rodríguez, Edgardo Moreno, Fabio Rodríguez y un conscripto clase 61.
> Edgardo Moreno, murió el domingo 2 de mayo de 1982, cuando el ARA Belgrano se hundió.
>
> Fotografía enviada por Carlos Rodríguez
> Ciudad de Buenos Aires

Absences

The sailors practised what to do in case they had to abandon ship. But during the war, not even that saved them.

From right to left, there are Carlos Rodríguez, Edgardo Moreno, Fabio Rodríguez and a conscript from class 61.

Edgardo Moreno died on Sunday, May 2, 1982, when the ARA Belgrano sank.

Foto con Víctor

"Acá estoy con el soldado Víctor Rodríguez, del Regimiento 7 que falleció en Malvinas. Hay dos Víctor Rodríguez fallecidos. Uno tiene su tumba identificada en Darwin, este es el otro". (Víctor es el más bajo)

Fotografía enviada por Antonio Reda
La Plata, Pcia. de Buenos Aires

Photo with Victor

"Here I am with him, Victor Rodriguez, of the 7th Regiment who died in the Falklands. There are two Victor Rodriguez deceased. One has his tomb identified in Darwin, this is the other. (Victor is the shortest)

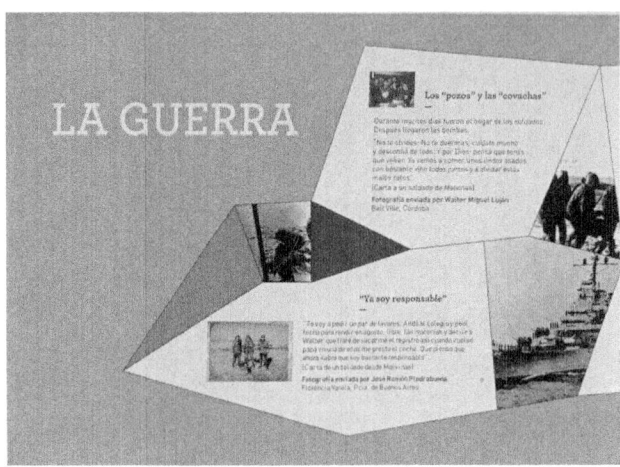

THE WAR

"Ya soy responsable"

"Te voy a pedir un par de favores. Andá al colegio y pedí fecha para rendir en agosto, libre, las materias y decile a Walter que trate de sacarme el registro así cuando vuelvo papá en una de esas me presta el coche. Que pienso que ahora sabrá que soy bastante responsable".
(Carta de un soldado desde Malvinas)

Fotografía enviada por José Ramón Piedrabuena
Florencia Varela, Pcia. de Buenos Aires

"I'm already responsible"
"I'm going to ask you for a couple of favours.

Go to school and ask for a date in August, to restart my subjects and tell Walter to try to get me registered, when I come back dad will lend me the car.

I think you now know that I am quite responsible."
(Letter from a soldier from the Falklands)

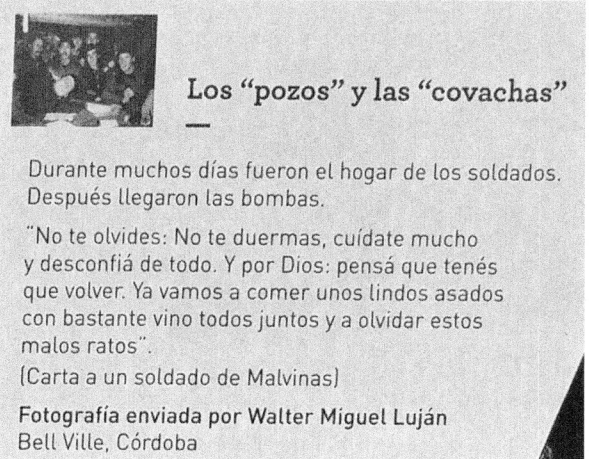

Los "pozos" y las "covachas"

Durante muchos días fueron el hogar de los soldados. Después llegaron las bombas.

"No te olvides: No te duermas, cuídate mucho y desconfiá de todo. Y por Dios: pensá que tenés que volver. Ya vamos a comer unos lindos asados con bastante vino todos juntos y a olvidar estos malos ratos".
(Carta a un soldado de Malvinas)

Fotografía enviada por Walter Miguel Luján
Bell Ville, Córdoba

The "wells" and the "ditches"
For many days was the home of the soldiers.
Then the bombs came.

"Don't forget: Don't fall asleep, take care of yourself a lot and be suspicious of everything. And by God, he thought you had to go back. We're going to eat some nice roasts with enough wine together and forget these bad times."

(Letter of a Falklands soldier)

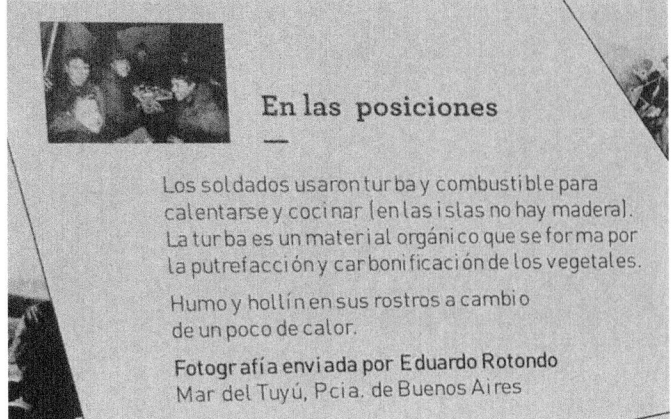

En las posiciones

Los soldados usaron turba y combustible para calentarse y cocinar (en las islas no hay madera). La turba es un material orgánico que se forma por la putrefacción y carbonificación de los vegetales.

Humo y hollín en sus rostros a cambio de un poco de calor.

Fotografía enviada por Eduardo Rotondo
Mar del Tuyú, Pcia. de Buenos Aires

In the positions

Soldiers used peat and fuel to heat up and cook (on the islands there is no wood). Peat is an organic material that is formed by the rot and carbonisation of vegetables.

Smoke and soot on their faces in exchange for a little heat.

Heridas

Hay heridas en el cuerpo y heridas en el alma.

Fotografía enviada por Carlos Mercante
La Plata, Pcia. de Buenos Aires

Wounds

There are wounds on the body and wounds on the soul.

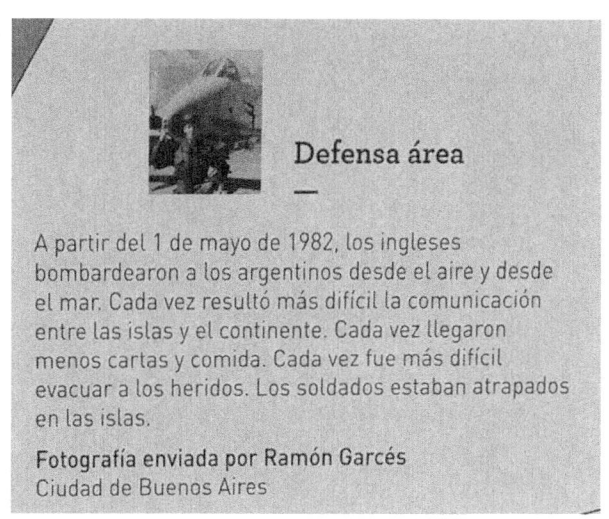

> **Defensa área**
>
> A partir del 1 de mayo de 1982, los ingleses bombardearon a los argentinos desde el aire y desde el mar. Cada vez resultó más difícil la comunicación entre las islas y el continente. Cada vez llegaron menos cartas y comida. Cada vez fue más difícil evacuar a los heridos. Los soldados estaban atrapados en las islas.
>
> **Fotografía enviada por Ramón Garcés**
> Ciudad de Buenos Aires

Defence area

As of May 1, 1982, the English bombed the Argentines from the air and the sea. Communication between the islands and the continent became increasingly difficult. Fewer and fewer letters and food arrived. It was becoming increasingly difficult to evacuate the wounded. The soldiers were trapped on the islands.

> **Hacia Malvinas**
>
> ¿Qué esperaban que les iba a suceder?
> ¿Se puede reír durante la guerra? ¿De qué?
> ¿Se puede reír después?
>
> **Fotografía enviada por Jorge Eduardo Rey**
> La Plata, Pcia. de Buenos Aires

Towards Falklands
What did you expect to happen to them?
Can you laugh during the war? About what?
Can you laugh later?

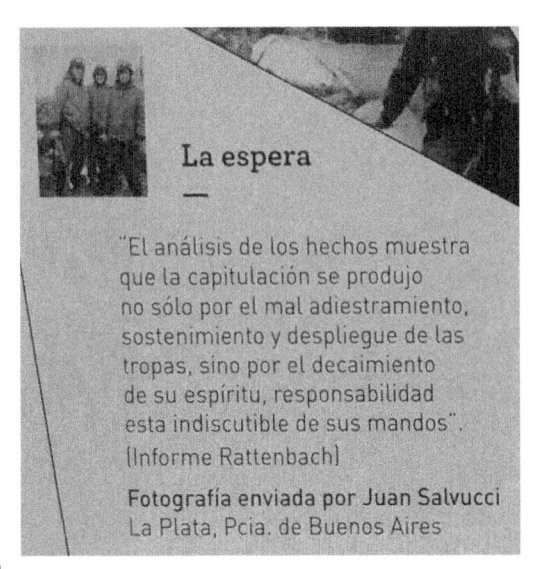

> **La espera**
>
> "El análisis de los hechos muestra que la capitulación se produjo no sólo por el mal adiestramiento, sostenimiento y despliegue de las tropas, sino por el decaimiento de su espíritu, responsabilidad esta indiscutible de sus mandos".
> (Informe Rattenbach)
>
> Fotografía enviada por Juan Salvucci
> La Plata, Pcia. de Buenos Aires

The wait

"The analysis of the facts shows that the capitulation was caused not only by the poor training, sustainability and deployment of the troops but by the decline of their spirit, responsibility is indisputable of their commanders."

(Rattenbach Report)

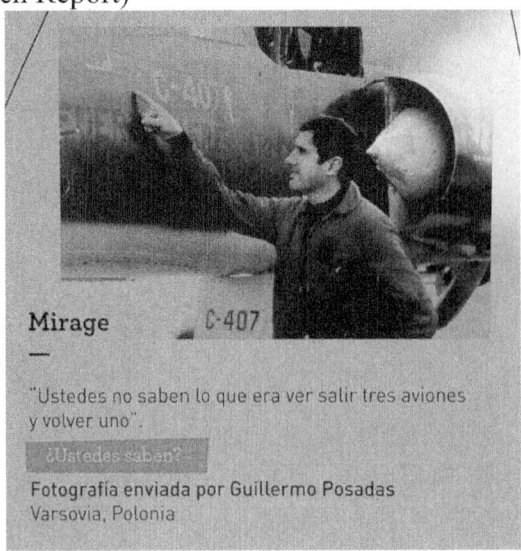

> **Mirage** C-407
>
> "Ustedes no saben lo que era ver salir tres aviones y volver uno".
> ¿Ustedes saben?
>
> Fotografía enviada por Guillermo Posadas
> Varsovia, Polonia

Mirage

"You don't know what it was like to see three planes go out and one come back."

Do you know?

(Many of the British forces know exactly what this means, it is difficult to know who the comments are aimed at but most likely it is for the general public to think about.)

> **En vuelo**
>
> ¿Cómo viajaron a Malvinas?
> ¿Habían tomado antes un avión?
> ¿Era necesaria una guerra para que lo conocieran?
>
> Fotografía enviada por José Héctor Bazán
> Verónica, Pcia. de Buenos Aires

In-flight
How did you travel to the Falklands?
Had they taken a plane before?
Was it a necessary war for them to meet him?

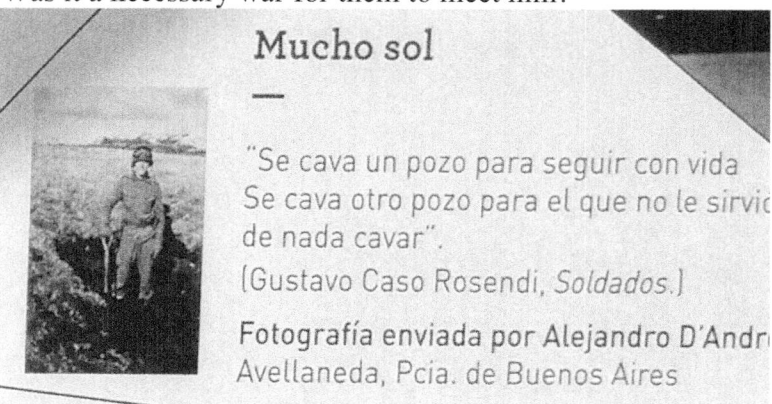

> **Mucho sol**
>
> "Se cava un pozo para seguir con vida
> Se cava otro pozo para el que no le sirvió
> de nada cavar".
> (Gustavo Caso Rosendi, *Soldados*.)
>
> Fotografía enviada por Alejandro D'Andr
> Avellaneda, Pcia. de Buenos Aires

Much sun

"A hole is dug to stay alive in.
Digging another hole for which it is of no use to dig".

1 + 1 + 1 + 1 + 1...

Si sumamos todos los alumnos de los años "A" y "B" de una escuela primaria, son más o menos 300 chicos por turno. Cuando los ingleses hundieron el ARA Belgrano, el 2 de mayo de 1982, hundieron tres escuelas y media. Y mataron una escuela entera: 323 marinos argentinos.

Fotografía enviada por Carlos Rodríguez
Ciudad de Buenos Aires

1 + 1 + 1 + 1 + 1...

If we add up all the pupils of the years "A" and "B" of an elementary school, it is about 300 boys per term. When the English sank the ARA Belgrano on 2 May 1982, they sank three and a half schools. They killed an entire school: 323 Argentine sailors.

Misa de campaña

Durante la guerra de Malvinas la canción de León Gieco "Sólo le pido a Dios" tuvo una gran popularidad. El músico la había compuesto años atrás, cuando existió la amenaza de un enfrentamiento con Chile.

¿Desde cuándo Argentina se preparaba para una guerra?

Fotografía enviada por Eduardo Rotondo
Mar del Tuyú, Pcia. de Buenos Aires

Campaign Mass

During the Falklands War, Leon Gieco's song "I only ask God" was very popular. The musician had composed it years ago when there was a threat of a confrontation with Chile.

Since when was Argentina prepared for war?

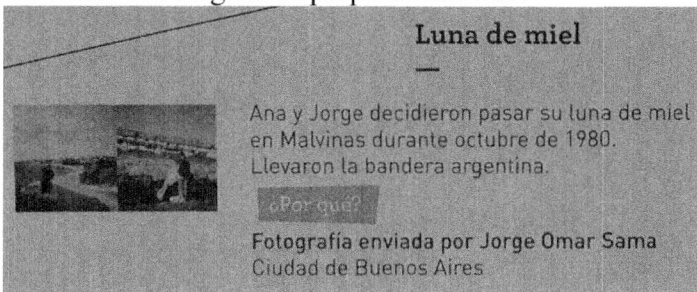

> **Luna de miel**
>
> Ana y Jorge decidieron pasar su luna de miel en Malvinas durante octubre de 1980. Llevaron la bandera argentina.
>
> ¿Por qué?
>
> Fotografía enviada por Jorge Omar Sama
> Ciudad de Buenos Aires

Honeymoon

Ana and Jorge decided to spend their honeymoon in the Falklands during October 1980.

They carried the Argentinian flag.

Why?

> **La "colimba"**
>
> "Corre, limpia y barre" era el nombre popular del Servicio Militar Obligatorio. Por una ley de 1901, generaciones de jóvenes argentinos cumplieron con ese deber cívico.
>
> Fotografía enviada por Nicolás Ivar Romero
> Villa Dolores, Córdoba

The "colimba"

"Run, clean and sweep" was the popular number during Obligatory Military Service. By a 1901 law, generations of young Argentines fulfilled that civic duty.

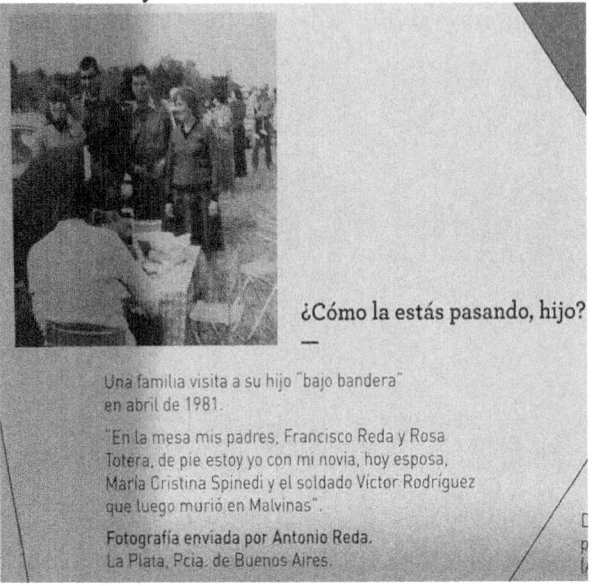

¿Cómo la estás pasando, hijo?

Una familia visita a su hijo "bajo bandera" en abril de 1981.

"En la mesa mis padres, Francisco Reda y Rosa Totera, de pie estoy yo con mi novia, hoy esposa, María Cristina Spinedi y el soldado Victor Rodríguez que luego murió en Malvinas".

Fotografía enviada por Antonio Reda.
La Plata, Pcia. de Buenos Aires.

Are you having a good time, son?

A family visits their son "under the flag" in April 1981.

"At the table, my parents, Francisco Reda and Rosa Totera standing with my girlfriend, today wife, María Cristina Spinedi and private Victor Rodríguez who later died in the Falklands".

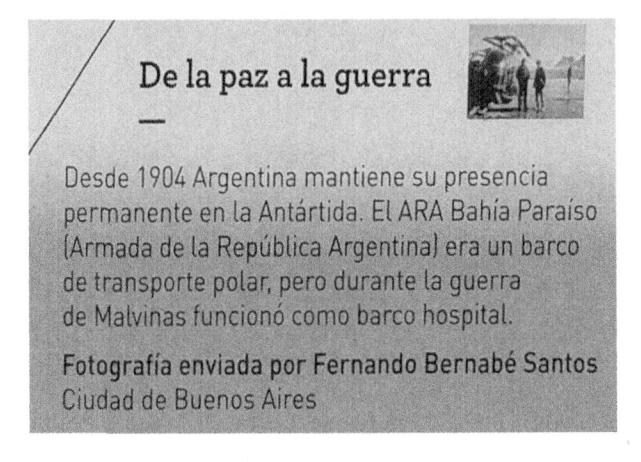

De la paz a la guerra

Desde 1904 Argentina mantiene su presencia permanente en la Antártida. El ARA Bahía Paraíso (Armada de la República Argentina) era un barco de transporte polar, pero durante la guerra de Malvinas funcionó como barco hospital.

Fotografía enviada por Fernando Bernabé Santos
Ciudad de Buenos Aires

From peace to war

Since 1904 Argentina maintains its permanent presence in Antarctica. The ARA Bahía Paraíso (Armada of the Argentine Republic) was a polar transport ship, but during the Falklands War, it functioned as a hospital ship

Fruta fresca

Las Malvinas están a menos de una hora de vuelo del continente. Durante la década de 1970, había vuelos semanales desde Comodoro Rivadavia. Las islas nunca estuvieron tan cerca: muchos isleños conocieron la fruta fresca por primera vez.

Fotografía enviada por María Fernanda Cañás
Ciudad de Buenos Aires

Fresh fruit

The Falklands are less than an hour's flight from the mainland. During the 1970s, there were weekly flights from Comodoro Rivadavia. The islands were never so close: many islanders first knew fresh fruit.

¡Mirá dónde estoy!

"La deuda interna" (1988) es una película que cuenta la historia de un joven de la puna, Verónico Cruz, que murió como tripulante del ARA General Belgrano durante la guerra de Malvinas. Nunca había visto el mar.

Fotografía enviada por Carlos Rodriguez
Ciudad de Buenos Aires

Look where I am!
"Internal Debt" (1988) is a film that tells the story of a young man of the country, Veronico Cruz, who died as a crewman of the ARA General Belgrano during the Falklands War. I've never seen the sea.

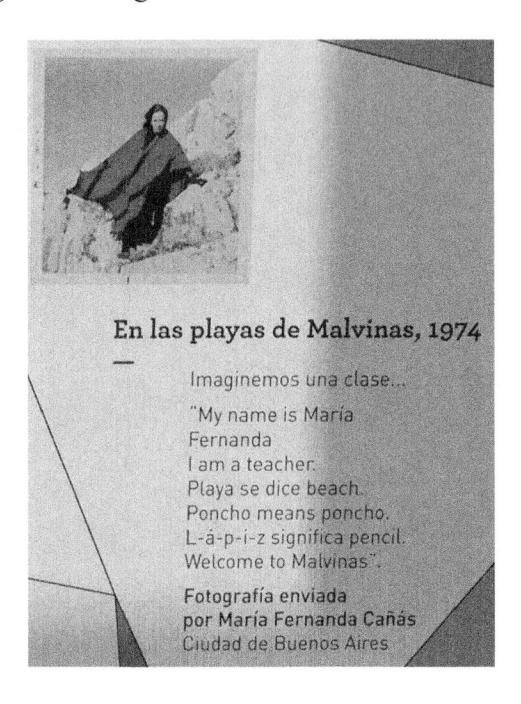

En las playas de Malvinas, 1974

Imaginemos una clase...

"My name is María Fernanda
I am a teacher.
Playa se dice beach.
Poncho means poncho.
L-á-p-i-z significa pencil.
Welcome to Malvinas".

Fotografía enviada por María Fernanda Cañás
Ciudad de Buenos Aires

On the beaches of Falklands, 1974
Imagine a class...

"My name is Maria Fernanda I am a teacher. Playa is called a beach. Poncho means poncho. L-a-p-i-z means pencil. Welcome to Falklands".

(This is almost the best part of the museum. Unfortunately, the Argentine people do not listen to their veterans; they do not even support them as they should.

To hide this display away from general sight is a disgrace but its existence is a small step in the right direction.)

GEOGRAPHY, FLORA AND FAUNA (2)

Up the stairs on the second floor, we find the Geography, Flora and Fauna exhibits.

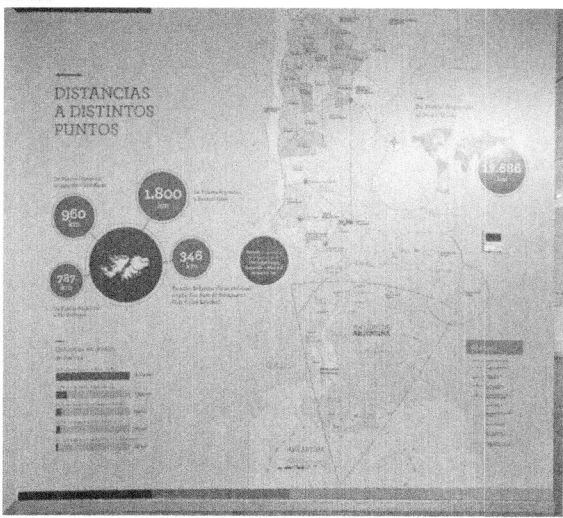

Next to that is a map showing how far away the islands are.

WE'RE IN THE FALKLANDS ISLANDS.

The most important natural resources are in the Argentine Sea.

The sea surrounding the archipelago is dominated by the Falklands marine current, a productive backbone of the Patagonian marine ecosystem.

The concentration of phytoplankton observed in the surroundings of the Falklands is among the highest in the Argentine Sea and supports, in turn, high densities of zooplankton.

The most important crustacean that navigates these waters with its light is krill.

The marine wealth is complemented by dense populations of squid, squid and fish: bass, sardine fueguina, hake, southern and Polish cod.

Non-renewable natural resources in the South Atlantic Ocean include potential hydrocarbon reserves.

That's the Falklands Islands.

Falklands soil

Economic activity on island soil: the main activity is sheep farming for wool export.

The first sheep of the Argentine colony was introduced by Governor Luis Vernet.

WE'RE IN THE FALKLAND ISLANDS.

From the mid-1700s, sea wolf hunters arrived. There were massacres of 800 animals a day. Under the Argentine flag, the controls were tighter and the populations recovered.

(There is no evidence of this.)

After the English colonial usurpation of 1833, they over-saw the hunters and the predation. In 1908 there were almost no sea lions.

The worst of all the killings was that of the Falklands fox, the only native mammal in our Islands. He was a meek fox who was a friend of man. He was exterminated by the British for considering him a plague that threatened cattle.

Today the predation continues at sea. Fishing is the most exploited resource and the core of economic activity.

The United Kingdom grants illegitimate fishing exploitation licences to large foreign companies.

That's what the Falkland Islands are like.

(Fishing licences have saved the Falklands, providing a good income for the islanders for the first time and some growth in the population.

The fishing is tightly controlled to sustain the sea life which is better than would have happened under Argentinian rule.)

Fishing predation

Squid make up 75% of fishing in 2012. 118 foreign vessels caught squid worth more than USD 1.6 billion. They capture 50 tons a day.

Oil Exploring

Potential hydrocarbon reserves is a new looting and new British colonial provocation, as well as a lethal threat to the environment.

(Yet more inflammatory words that only serve to educate a public that knows little better I am afraid.)

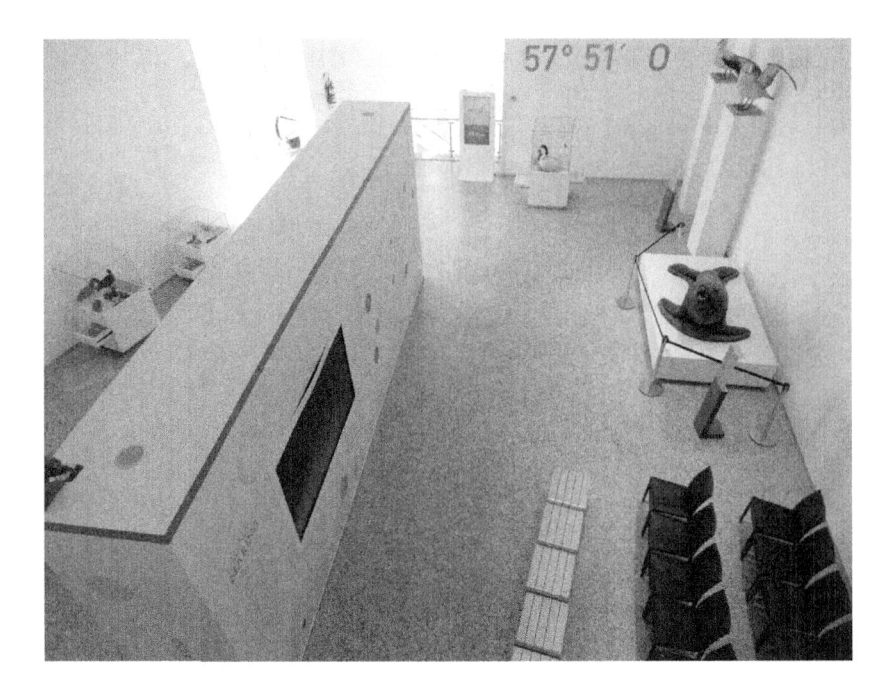

Looking down from the upper floor onto the whole area with a few scruffy specimens of the local wildlife.

(Given that Puerto Madryn is a huge Argentinian wildlife reserve you would have thought they could have filled this section with exhibits because some of the wildlife is common to both areas.)

RAYMUNDO GLEYZER (3)

I did not find any information displayed in this section, perhaps I missed it although some exhibits have been removed from the museum. I have included some notes anyway because he was significant, both in the work that he did and as a reminder to the people of Argentina of what happened to him.

Raymundo Gleyzer was born in Buenos Ares on 25th September 1941 and has been missing since May 27th 1976, one of the disappeared.

This Argentine political filmmaker specialized in documentaries and he was an opponent of the military dictatorship and so he was most likely murdered.

Part of a Jewish family he had a great interest in film and politics, so much so that all of his films fought social injustices and favoured revolution.

The backward northeast of Brazil was the location of his first film where he was almost murdered. Then in the early 1970's he created "The Frozen Revolution" which depicted the failure of The Mexico Revolution and the film was banned in Argentina.

He was a co-founder of the Cine de las Base group that organised demonstrations by workers in all walks of life.

The "Traitors" was his last major film which criticised the Perónists politicians who played an important role in 1973 Argentina. In it, he claims that the leaders have allied themselves with outside powers to enrich themselves and stay in power, so in other words, there is a corrupt government system.

The Junta came into power in March 1976 and one of their death squads abducted him on May 27, 1976. It is believed that he was tortured and murdered.

ROOM (4)

NAUTICAL TRIPS

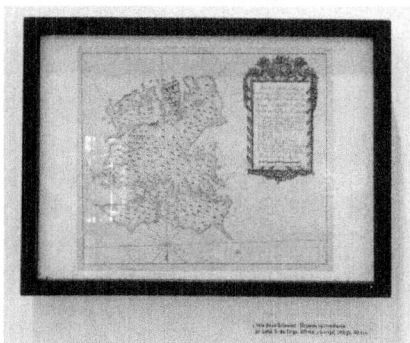

Falkland Island Meridian location.

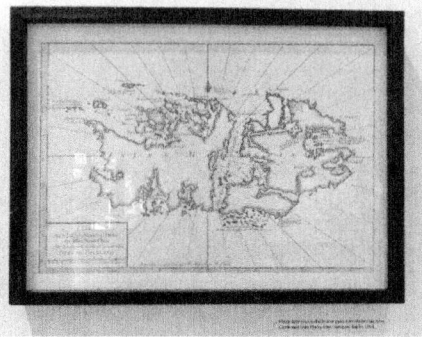

Map testimony of the brief French passage through the Islands.
Carte des Isles Malouines. Jacques Belli. 1764

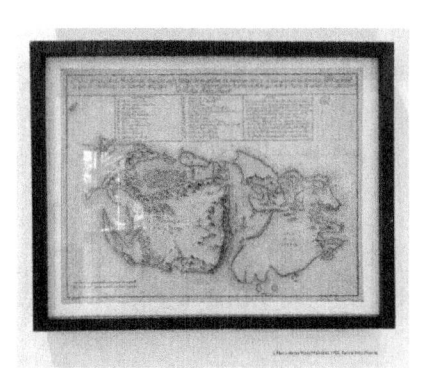

Plan of the Falkland Islands.1769
Felipe Ruiz Puente

Description of the Eastern Coast of Patagonia. 1779

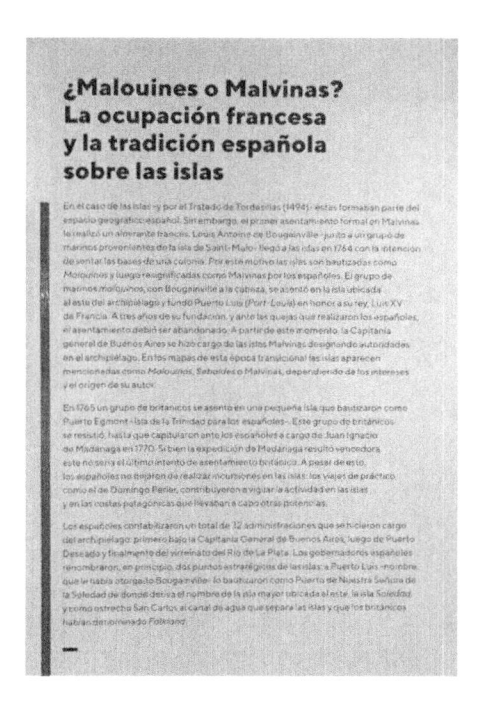

Malouines or Falklands?

The French occupation and the Spanish tradition on the islands.

In the case of the islands - and by the Treaty of Tordesillas (1494) - these were part of the Spanish geographical area.

However, the first formal settlement in the Falklands was made by a French admiral. Louis Antoine de Bougainville - together with a group of sailors from the island of Saint-Malo - arrived on the islands in 1764 intending to lay the foundations of a colony. For this reason, the islands are named Malouines and then translated by the Spanish. The group of Malouian sailors, with Bougainville at the helm, settled on the island located east of the archipelago and founded Port Louis in honour of King, Louis XV of France. Three years after its founding, and in the face of complaints made by the Spaniards, the settlement had to be abandoned. From this moment on, the General Captaincy of Buenos Aires took over the Falkland Islands by appointing authorities.

¿Sabías que...

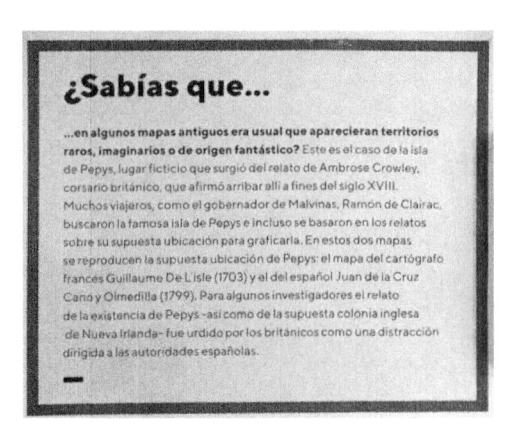

...en algunos mapas antiguos era usual que aparecieran territorios raros, imaginarios o de origen fantástico? Este es el caso de la isla de Pepys, lugar ficticio que surgió del relato de Ambrose Crowley, corsario británico, que afirmó arribar allí a fines del siglo XVIII. Muchos viajeros, como el gobernador de Malvinas, Ramón de Clairac, buscaron la famosa isla de Pepys e incluso se basaron en los relatos sobre su supuesta ubicación para graficarla. En estos dos mapas se reproducen la supuesta ubicación de Pepys: el mapa del cartógrafo francés Guillaume De L'isle (1703) y el del español Juan de la Cruz Cano y Olmedilla (1799). Para algunos investigadores el relato de la existencia de Pepys –así como de la supuesta colonia inglesa de Nueva Irlanda– fue urdido por los británicos como una distracción dirigida a las autoridades españolas.

Did you know that...... on some ancient maps, it was common for territories to appear weird, imaginary or of fantastic origin? This is the case for the island of Pepys, a fictional place that arose from the account of Ambrose Crowley, British privateer, who claimed to arrive beyond the end of the 15th century.

Many travellers, such as the governor of Falklands, Ramon de Clairac, searched for the famous island of Pepys and even relied on the stories about its supposed location to graph it. On these two maps Pepys' supposed location is reproduced: the map of the cartographer Guillaume De Líisle (1703) and that of the Spaniard Juan de la Cruz Cano and Olmedilla (1799). For some researchers, the story of Pepys's existence - as well as the alleged English colony of New Ireland -- was warped by the British as a distraction addressed to the Spanish authorities.

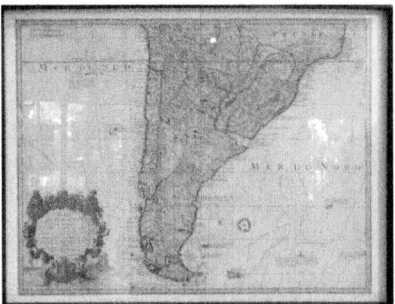

POLITICAL TRADITIONS

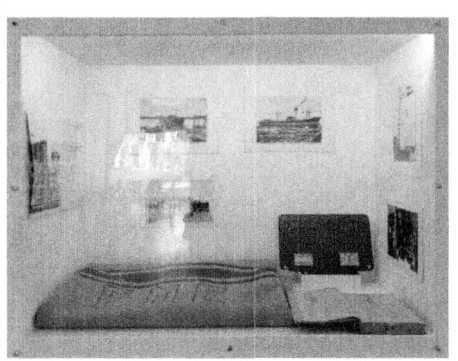

More than half of Argentina's production, especially cereals and meat, was through Great Britain. This country, which had the largest commercial fleet in the world, was also in a position, due to the volume of its export to Argentina and the size of its warehouses, to impose transport conditions. This economic dependence of Argentina with the exterior is a failing of the ruling class that ruled the country from the second half of the 19th century, who postponed improvements and did not carry out projects to reverse this situation, and did not to comply with the few laws when they were sanctioned."

PERÓN AND THE MARITIME POLICY IN ARGENTINA: THE STATE MERCHANT FLEET, 1946-1955

(Corruption at the highest levels has been an ongoing problem. Perón was no different from the rest; Eva went to Switzerland and opened bank accounts there.

Argentina did quite well during this period financially but the corruption continued and maybe Nazi money had something to do with it. It was when Perón and Perónism took hold.

Over the coming years corruption continued and eventually, the countries debts started to pile up again.)

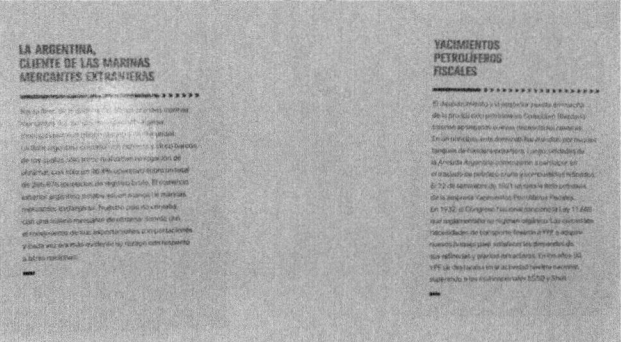

ARGENTINA, CUSTOMER OF FOREIGN MERCHANT MARINES

Towards the end of the decade of the 30 great merchant navies of the world, the English especially monopolized the marine trade worldwide. The Argentine fleet had eighty-five ships, of which only thirteen carried out overseas sailing, with only 26.4% operational on a total of 265,678 tones gross registration. Argentine foreign trade was thus in the hands of foreign merchant navies. Our country did not have an overseas merchant navy in line with the movement of its exports and imports and its lag to other nations was becoming increasingly evident.

YACIMIENTOS PETROLIFEROS FISCALES

The discovery and subsequent commissioning of oil production in Comodoro Rivadavia would bring new shipping needs. Initially, this demand was met by foreign-flagged tankers. Argentine Navy units then began to participate in the transfer of crude oil and refined fuels. On September 22, 1921, the oil fleet of the company Yacimientos Petrolíferos Fiscales was created. In 1932, the National Congress passed Law 11.668 regulating its organic regime. A growing transportation need did lead the YPF to acquire new vessels to meet the demands of its refineries and extraction plants. In the 1950s, YPF excelled in national shipping activity, beating the multinationals ESSO and Shell.

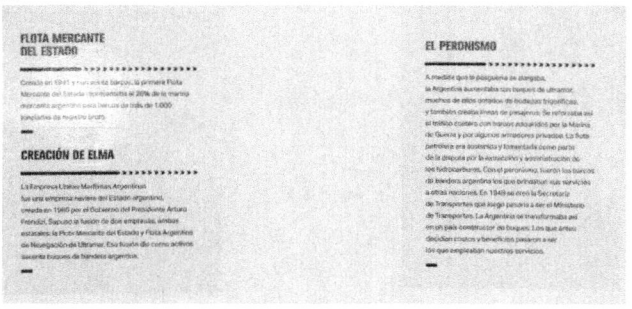

FLOTA MERCANTE DEL ESTADO (STATE MERCHANT FLEET)

Created in 1941 and with twenty ships, the first Merchant Fleet of the State accounted for 26% of the Argentine merchant navy of ships with more than 1,000 tons of gross registration.

CREATION OF ELMA

The Empresa Lineas Maritimas Argentinas was a shipping company of the Argentine State, created in 1960 by the government of President Arturo Frondizi. It involved the merger of two companies, both state-owned: the State Merchant Fleet and the Argentine Overseas Sailing Fleet. Sixty Argentine-flagged vessels were active.

PERÓNISM

As the post-war period lengthened, Argentina increased its overseas vessels; many of them equipped with refrigeration, and also created passenger lines. Coastal traffic was thus reinforced by ships purchased by the Navy and some private ship owners. The oil fleet was sustained and encouraged as part of the dispute over the extraction and administration of hydrocarbons. With Perónism, it was the Argentine-flagged ships that provided their services to other nations. In 1948 the Secretary of Transportation was created, which would later become the Ministry of Transportation. Argentina thus transformed into a shipbuilding country. Those who previously decided on costs and benefits became the ones who used our services.

ANTARES

Being governor for three periods of Tierra del Fuego, Ernesto Manuel Campos carried out works that seemed impossible for the time. He managed to recognize and overcome many of the transport, health and supply limitations that complicated the daily life of the Fuegians. With the active cooperation of YPF, he developed the Antares Project, which consisted of the construction of the fuel storage and distribution plant on the islands. Thanks to the interest and work of Campos, the Falklands Islands managed to break the isolation to which the British Crown condemned them. During that moment in our history, the islands and the continent maintained intense commercial traffic.

THE NATIONAL NAUTICAL SCHOOL OF MANUEL BELGRANO

It incorporated the first group of women into its courses in 1978, making our country a pioneer in the training and incorporation of merchant officer women.

DECADE OF 90

After the Falklands War, ELMA suffered its first reduction. In 1989, it had a fleet of thirty-six general cargo ships. The 1990s began with the privatization of many of the services offered by the National State. ELMA was no exception. Their most important ships were put up for sale. Several of them were acquired by companies or nations that formed consortia that competed on the same shipping routes as

Argentine-flagged vessels. During 1995 the liquidation of units continued and in March 1996 despite keeping four container ships and two refrigerators in operation, discontinuation was decided. In 1997, the last six ships were sold and ELMA disappeared as a company.

RELATIONSHIP WITH GREAT BRITAIN

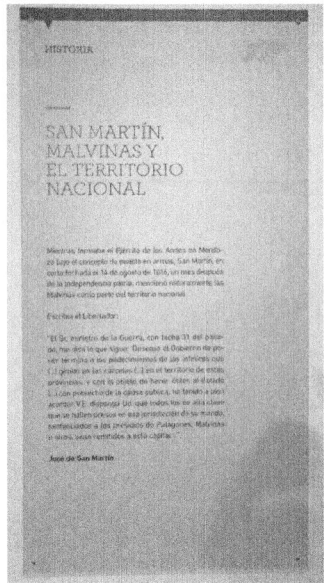

HISTORY
SAN MARTIN, FALKLANDS AND THE NATIONAL TERRITORY

While training the Army of the Andes in Mendoza under the concept of people-in-arms, Saint Martin, in a letter dated August 14, 1816, a month after the Independence homeland, naturally mentioned the Falklands as part of the national territory.

The Liberator wrote:

"Mr Minister of War, dated 31 of the past, tells me the following: 'I wish the Government to put an end to the sufferings of the unhappy who (...) they groan in prisons (...) in the territory of these provinces, and to make them useful to the State (...) for the benefit of the public cause, you have agreed to agree that you provide that all high-class prisoners in that jurisdiction of your command, sentenced to be prisoners of Patagones, Falklands or others, be referred to this capital...'".

José de San Martín

(This appears to be here because it mentions the Falklands but has no relevance to the islands.)

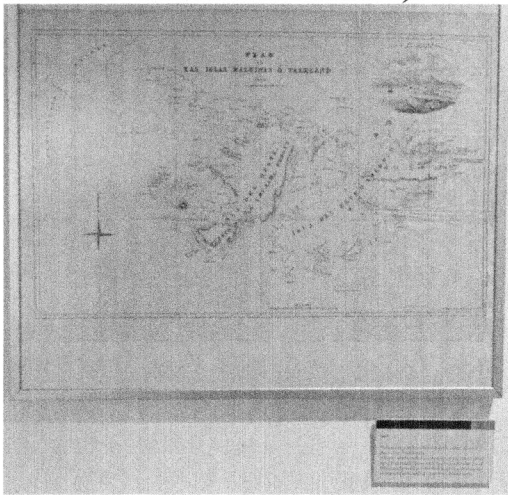

English map of the Falkland Islands in 1841 with a drawing of Puerto Louis (Isla Soledad)
William Langdon received a grant from Luis Vernet and made this drawing titled "A View of Port Louis, Berkeley Sound". This drawing was included in the claim brochure of the Argentine government, presented by Jose Maria Moreno in 1841.

Above: Gaucho methods of driving wild horses are described.
Below: view of Puerto Guillermo (Bahia de Stanley).
Images and text published in a British magazine of the time, where it is mentioned that the Falklands Islands were incorporated in 1845 as a British colony.

(William Langdon was a British Naval officer and they were all trained as surveyors and mapmakers, of course, Vernet paid him to do this work but it has nothing to do with any sovereignty claim.)

FIRST ENGLISH INVASION: 1806

British troops landed on 24 June 1806 at the port of Ensenada under the command of Capt.-Tan Beresford. Spanish viceroy Sobremonte began the withdrawal. For 46 days the English occupied Buenos Aires. Santiago de Liniers, in charge of Spanish and Creole troops, and Buenos Aires urban militias, reconquered Buenos Aires.

SECOND ENGLISH INVASION: 1807

10,000 soldiers commanded by the British captain Whitelocke landed on 4 July 1807 in Ensenada and marched to Plaza Miserere. The Porteños resisted with 9000 militiamen under Martín de Alzaga. The population defended themselves by throwing water and boiling oil against the occupation forces. On July 7, Whitelocke surrendered to Liniers.

Anglo-French blockade

Between 1845 and 1850, the Argentine Confederation was blockaded. The two countries sought to dismiss Juan Manuel de Rosas to establish free trade in our inland rivers.

Vuelta de Obligado

On November 20, 1845, the battle of the Vuelta de Obligado was fought on the Paraná River. The Argentines, commanded by Gen. Lucio Manilla, crossed swords on the river and resisted heroically.

National Sovereignty
For this episode, the Liberator San Martin bequeathed his sabre to Brigadier Juan Manuel de Rosas. On November 20, National day was declared.

(No mention of the fact that the fleet was a combined British and French fleet.)

LA BARING BROTHERS, 1824
The Governor of Buenos Aires Martín Rodríguez, at the suggestion of Minister Bernardino Rivadavia, borrowed one million pounds with Banca Baring Brothers. Thus began the process of Argentine external indebtedness. The Baring borrowing was settled a hundred and twenty-three years later during the first government of Perón in 1947.

PACTO ROCA-RUNCIMAN, 1933
The global financial crisis of 1929 reduced the income-ability of English businesses in Argentina.

Both governments signed in London the Roca-Runciman Pact: Great Britain would buy Argentine meat in exchange for tax exemption, for use in British fridges and granting of the monopoly of public transport in Buenos Aires to an English corporation.

Complaint
The Roca-Runciman Pact was denounced for fraud and transfer of sovereignty.

LA FORESTAL
Until the first half of the twentieth century, the British Empire maintained colonial conduct with Argentina. With the extraction of tannin in the north of Santafesino and the devastating logging of the ravine, the company La Forestal exercised an indiscriminate power over labourers and traders.

(The local Argentinian Governor Enrique Mosca was fully involved in this, no doubt lining his own pockets.)

LOS FERROCARRILES
The fan-shaped layout of the British railways, from the periphery to the Port of Buenos Aires, made them an instrument of domination, as stated by Raul Scalabrini Ortiz.

LA PATAGONIA AND THE BANK
The exploitation of sheep in Patagonia and the financial control of local banking and the Central Bank were the other chapter of domination, in partnership with local oligarchic sectors.
(Note: this is in partnership with locals, more corruption.)

The British community
Is integrated into Argentine society.

The Welsh community in Patagonia, the practice of soccer, polo, hockey, and the British ancestry of personalities such as Jorge Luis Borges and Maria Elena Walsh bear witness to this.

(Jorge Luis Borges father was half British, part Spanish and part Portuguese, his mother was Spanish, Maria Elena Walsh had Irish ancestry.)

The Tragic Rebellion
The rebellion of the workers in the Santa Cruz ranches was the tragic prelude to the decline of British rule.

(300 striking peasant workers were killed by the Argentinian Army in the rebellion which started in 1920 and ended in 1922. This has absolutely nothing to do with Britain, yet another attempt to blame anyone else but especially the British. In reality, this is another example of barbaric Argentinian rule.)

Perónism
The nationalization of the railways and the cancellation of the external debt during the Perónist government meant the definitive retreat of the British Empire in Argentina.

BIOGRAPHIES (5)

ANTONIO EL GAUCHO RIVIERO

He was born on November 7, 1808, in Concepción del Uruguay, Entre Ríos. It was a rural place *(Fue peon rural)*. He travelled to the Falklands Islands in 1826 along with the merchant Luis Vernet. The foreigners nicknamed him "Antook", to the others he was El Gaucho Rivero.

When on January 3, 1833, the English usurped our Islands, Rivero wanted to resist and refused to return to Buenos Aires with the sailor Pinedo. He stayed in the Falklands with a few colonists, Indians, blacks, and gauchos.

With the Argentine population already evicted, Rivero defended the national pride. So until August 26, 1833, he headed the rebellion.

There were three creoles and five Indian crerules. They lowered the English flag and raised the blue and white flag. There were deaths and injuries.

Resisting in the Falklands

In January 1834, he was imprisoned. After questioning him, he was released into the Rio de la Plata.

They say he died fighting in the Vuelta de Obligado on November 20, 1845.

(This is the Argentinian hero who was a murderer of their people. Is he another Galtieri perhaps?)

PERÓN
AND THE FALKLANDS

THE MANDATE OF SOVEREIGNTY

During his mandate, the main public services were nationalized, created and strengthened: Railways, Airlines, Mail, Merchant Marine, Telephony, Electricity and others.

He was the first democratic president to present the Falklands Question to the UN.

In 1947 the TIAR was born and managed to make the Continental Security zone include Falklands, Georgia and Sandwich Islands.
(TIAR is the Inter-American Treaty of Reciprocal Assistance)
(During the Falklands War (1982), the United States favoured the United Kingdom because Argentina had been the aggressor and because Argentina had not been attacked, as did Chile and Colombia. This was seen by most Latin American countries as the final failure of the treaty.)

On November 30, 1973, promulgates Law 20.561, which establishes June 10 as the Day of the Affirmation of Argentine Rights over the Falkland, Islands and Antarctic Sector.

In 1974, he instructed the Foreign Ministry to deepen agreements with the British government for sovereignty in the Falklands and to consolidate the presence of public companies on the islands.

The textbooks of Perónism exalted our sovereignty in Antarctica and the Falklands.

Perón said: "There are those who say that since Antarctica is a continuation of the Falklands, Antarctica also belongs to them. This reminds me of the case of a man who took a dog from my house and later made a lawsuit over the chain."

Biography
He was born in Lobos, Buenos Aires province, on October 8, 1895.
As a military man, he reaches the highest grade: Lieutenant General.
Political life
Leader and head of the political movement created by him and Maria Eva Duarte, Evita, from the popular mobilization of October 17, 1945.

Elected President by popular vote in three terms 1946, 1952 (overthrown in 1955 by a civil-military coup) and 1973.

The flags of Political Sovereignty, Social Justice and Economic Independence identified his doctrine.

He died on July 1, 1974.

HISTORY
ARGENTINE FLAG THAT FLAMED IN THE FALKLAND ISLANDS

September 28, 1966: 17 young people led by Dardo Cabo formed The Condor Operative.

They landed in Puerto Rivero, Falklands Islands, aboard a plane of Aerolíneas Argentinas hijacked during a flight Buenos Aires-Río Gallegos, Santa Cruz. They raised seven Argentine flags and sang our national anthem.

This is one of those flags.

Expelled by the English, they were arrested at the arrival on the continent by the dictatorship of Onganía.

Hidden since then, the seven flags were delivered by María Cristina Verrier, the only woman of the Condor Group, to President Cristina Fernández de Kirchner for custody.

Dardo Cabo was assassinated by the dictatorship in 1977.

1   Photographs linked to the open case against the militants of "Operative Condor"

2   "PATRIA MIA" on Mount Longdon, Falklands Islands, September 2013.

A federal itinerant art installation designed with 200 meters of Argentine flag fabric.

Between 2010 — 2013 we travelled more than 45,000 km in national territory, reaching all Argentine provinces.

The Ora has written 6,000 messages in favour of the motherland.

Authors: Maride! Cano-Abel Acevedo. Departure from La Costa, Pcia from Buenos Aires, Argentina

3   Time passes, the Condor too, but unfolding and flying flags in the Falkland Islands continues.

Former combatants and their children in the Falklands, 2014.

THE 3 PLAZAS (6)

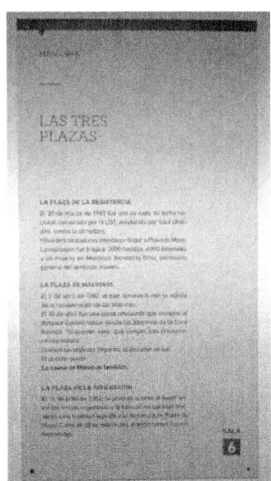

THE PLACE OF RESISTANCE

On March 30, 1982, it was a day of a national strike called by the CGT, led by Saúl Ubaldini, against the dictatorship.

Thousands of workers tried to reach the Plaza de Mayo. The repression was tragic: 2000 wounded, 4000 detainees and one killed in Mendoza: Benedicto Ortiz, general secretary of the mining union.

THE PLAZA DE FALKLANDS

On April 2, 1982, the country dawned to the news of the Falklands recovery.

On April 10th it was an overflowing square that heard dictator Galtieri speak from the balconies of Casa Rosada: "If they want to come, come. We will present them with battle." When the English arrived, the dictator left.

The town was left.

The cause of Falklands was too.

THE PLACE OF INDIGNATION

On 14 June 1982, Argentine and British troops in the Falkland Islands cease-fire. A crowd repudiated the dictatorship in Plaza de Mayo. Like on March 30, protesters were repressed.

THE GOOD "AND THE BETTER

FRAGMENT OF "ARGENTINA, YEARS OF CULTURAL WIRES" JULIO CORTÁZAP

"I will try to summarize in a few sentences a very complex question:

1
Argentines have never ceased to claim what they consider their rights to the Falkland Islands.
Consequently, and after many years of unsuccessful diplomatic claims before the British crown, the current "de facto" occupation of the islands is nothing more than the fulfilment of a will that has deep roots in the entire Argentine people.

2
If this can be considered logical and justified, the fact that the occupation has been decided and carried out by the military government of General Galtieri constitutes an act that the vast majority of international observers consider as a mere political manoeuvre, aimed at distracting the attention of the Argentines in front of the very serious situation that the country is going through.

3
This situation is the result of almost ten years of repression, murder and torture, and the disappearance of many people estimated to be between fifteen and thirty thousand, which has brought, among other dire consequences, the exile of hundreds of thousands of Argentines and a climate of insecurity, censorship and discouragement that is reflected throughout the country's landscape.

4
In recent years, this negative process has been a real economic catastrophe, with all its social and labour aspects of the country. Inflation, famine, wage freezes and many other factors of that order have created a climate of uncertainty that, in recent months, began to manifest itself in the form of public protests, and which culminated in a series of protests held in the streets of Buenos Aires, and the interior, very few days before the government decided to occupy the Falklands.

5
For all that, in the face of the chaotic situation in the country and the spectacular military operation that has just taken place, I think that if it is okay to liberate the Falkland Islands from English rule, much better would be to liberate all of Argentina from the dominance of its government regime.

"Only, naturally, those who have just done the first do not have the slightest intention of carrying out the Second"

JULIO CORTÁZAR

ROOM (7)

Walking up to the top floor on the stairs, I turned and photographed the atrium, down below is the central diorama with the blue circles and it gives an idea of the size of this exhibit.

Although this only shows the central part of the museum it does give an idea of how large it is, the top floor being mostly about the 1982 war.

Hanging above is the Cessna 185 named "Don Luis Vernet" which was flown to the Falkland Islands on September 8th 1964; I joined the Royal Navy on the same day. The pilot was Miguel Fitzgerald, born in Argentina to Irish parents on 8th September 1926 so it was his 38th birthday. He was to carry out a similar unauthorised flight 4 years later in November.

REPRESENTATIVE MODEL

**ARGENTINE COLONY IN PORT LOUIS
EAST FALKLAND. 1831**

This was Port Louis in the Falklands Islands.

There lived our gauchos and settlers inaugurating the homeland in the south of the continent.

Don Luis Vernet, his commander, snatched the cattle with his countrymen while guarding the coast against the attacks of foreign ships. It was a people of peace and various trades, made up of Creoles, Indians, blacks, Europeans and the gauchos of Rivero.

There those Argentines forged their lives until 1833. When British colonialism expelled them, those first settlers did not lower the blue and white flag.

(There is no information about this radar aerial or display).

LIFE IN WAR INSTALLATION

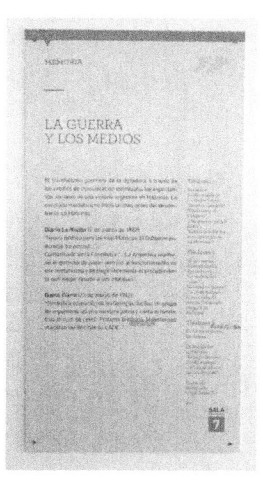

MEMORY
THE WAR AND THE MEDIA

The warlike triumphalism of the dictatorship through the media stimulated the social expectations of an Argentine victory in the Falklands. The media escalation began a month before the landing in Falklands.

La Nación Newspaper (March 2, 1982): "New policy for the Falkland Islands. The Government attitude...... Statement from the Chancellery: "... Argentina maintains the right to terminate the functioning of this mechanism and to freely choose the procedure that best suits its interests".

Clarín Newspaper (March 23, 1982).
"Symbolic occupation of South Georgia. A group of Argentines raised a national flag and sang the hymn, after which they withdrew. British protest. Islanders attacked LADE offices... ".

Headlines 1

During the armed conflict. the titles were: "We're winning." "Destroying the Canberra", "Glorious Day for the Homeland", "Euphoria popular for the recovery of the Falklands".

Headlines 2
"If they attack us, we will fight, Galtieri said," "The Victory of Courage," "Being at War," "The Board rejected Reagan's proposal. Imminent attack on the Falklands."

Headlines 3
Of such triumphalism, such defeat. The Nation of 15/06/1982: "A ceasefire has occurred and its conditions must be agreed."
Clarín headline of 18/06/1982: "Galtieri fell".

FALLS IN COMBAT

(The small amount of war paraphernalia, to the victor the spoils.)

POSTWAR PERIOD

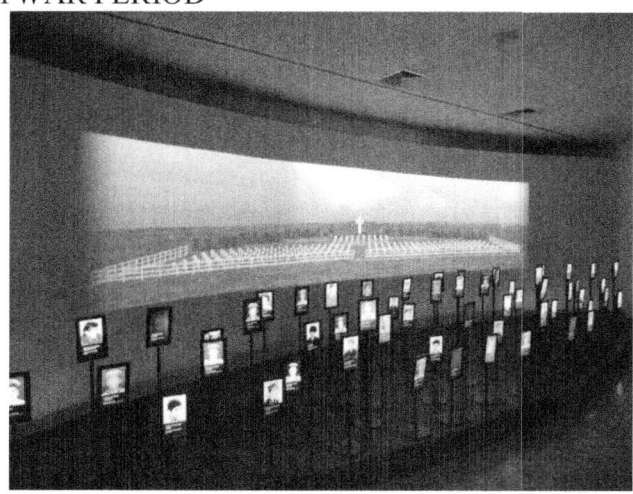

(I have visited this Argentine cemetery in the Falklands and this was a fitting display and tribute to the fallen. It is such a pity that it took the Argentine government so long to recognise that they need to take care of the veterans and their families by looking after this place in the Falklands.)

PEACE, MEMORY AND SOVEREIGNTY

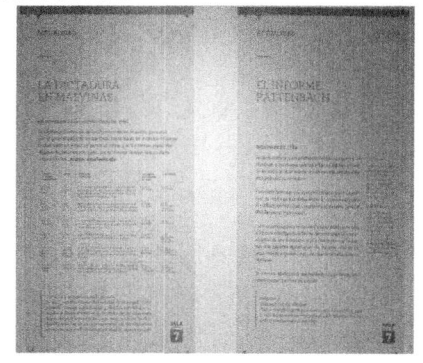

THE DICTATORSHIP IN FALKLANDS
THE COMMISSION CALVI, JUNE-JULY 1982

Commission for the Evaluation of Operations in The Falklands, chaired by General Edgardo Nestor Calvi, commander of Military Institutes. It evaluated 5000 reports of military personnel and 600 special reports. Some testimonies collected by the report reveal the treatment of soldiers. **Declassified File:**

TITLE AND NAME (REPORTED)	RANK	SUBSTANCE OF THE COMPLAINT	DOCUMENT RECORDING THE FACT	PROPOSAL
TTE 1RO BITTI RAFAEL	J SEC CA CDO RI 25	EL S/C 63 MARTINEGRO Edgardo j. He declares: Having received bad treatment (being tied hand and foot behind his back, placing him face down on the wet beach sand, from 9:00 to 17:00).	FICHA IND. NRO. 00188	EXPAND INVESTIGATION
SUBT. FLORES EDUARDO	J SEC CA "B" RI 3	EL S/S 61 MARTA Pedro declares: that the aforementioned official did not allow him to be attended to in the infirmary for trench foot and that, for eating a piece of lamb, he was staked.	FICHA IND. NRO. 00699	SUBTRACT TRANSCENDENCE EXPAND INVESTIGATION
CABO 1RO CANCINIO	J GPO CA "B" RI 3	EL S/C 61 MARTA Pedro declares: that the aforementioned non-commissioned officer beat him and urinated on his back, keeping him in a puddle for long hours.	FICHA IND. NRO. 00699	EXPAND INVESTIGATION
CABO 1RO GOMEZ	J GPO RI 4	EL S/C 63 PEREZ GRANDE Jorge declares that the aforementioned non-commissioned officer stole food from the soldiers.	FICHA IND. NRO. 00685	SUBTRACTING DECLARANT'S EXTENSION TRANSCENDENCE
CABO 1RO GALARZA MIGUEL ANGEL	J PELCDO 2RA SEC ING COMB 601	EL S/C 61 DI PIETRO Sergio Fabian declares: that the deceased exercised bad treatment with the troops and made a bad distribution of food, which he hoarded for personal consumption.	ACTA DE RECEEPCION NRO. 00001	DO NOT GIVE TRANSCENDENCE OF THE DECLARANT
MY. ENG. ETIENOT JORGE	J CA ING COMB 601	EL S/C 62 DE LUCA Antonio declares that when the enemy fire beat their positions, the J Ca fled in a jeep, abandoning the troops and NCOs.	ACTA DE RECEEPCION FOJA NRO. 28	DO NOT GIVE TRANSCENDENCE OF THE DECLARANT

(This Commission occurred in 1983/4 and was effectively a whitewash. Most of the complaints by men about how they were treated were dismissed and those which should have been looked into have had no action. I believe that the complaints were justified.)

RATTENBACH REPORT
DECEMBER 1982

Argentina was a country devastated by the war in the Falklands, the tragic consequences of state terrorism and the economic plan of deindustrialization imposed by the dictatorship.

To wash off its image, the Military Board appointed a military service officer's commission to prepare a report on the Falklands conflict. It was presided over by Lieutenant General (Re) Benjamin Rattenbach.

Contrary to the dictatorship's plans, the commission thoroughly investigated and concluded its report by demonstrating the failure of dictators and the serious harm it causes to the patient diplomacy that, for more than a century, Argentina did to regain sovereignty in the Falklands.

The Rattenbach report remained hidden as "state secret".

Report 3 Paragraph 787 of the report:

"The opportunity freely set by the Military Board for the recovery of the South Atlantic archipelago directly benefited to the enemy".

Report 1

The Siete Dias magazine, at the end of 1983, and the CECIM (Falkland Islands Ex-combatant Center), in La Plata, in 1988, released parts of that "secret".

Report 2

On February 7, 2012, President Cristina Fernandez de Kirchner ordered the declassification and dissemination within the framework of the Memory, Truth and Justice, Democracy and Sovereignty policy.

(The museum appears to have been inspired by this dangerous and opportunistic woman, see the next section. She seems to grasp every opportunity to look good by adopting seemingly good causes but where has her fortune come from? Her wealth is shown as $115million on the internet; it is likely much more, not bad for the daughter of a bus driver.

As I wander around the museum I start to wonder at how all this is being paid for in a country that has huge debts again.)

MEDIA SECTION (8)

"... Hoy Malvinas ha dejado de ser solamente una causa de los argentinos para transformarse en una causa global de América Latina..."

Presidenta de la Nación
Dra. Cristina Fernández de Kirchner

"... Today the Falklands have ceased to be only a cause of the Argentines and become a global cause of Latin America ..."

President of the Nation
Dr. Cristina Fernández de Kirchner

Slipping out of the door into the fresh air was a relief because none of the attendants took any notice of me. There had been one other visitor, a lady looking round; it seemed that she was being ignored as well.

For my walk back to the train I used the northern exit, just to confuse them and even stopped for a coke. I had to be back for 2 pm and even managed to go and have a look at Casa Rosada which was where Evita wowed the crowds, and as I journeyed back to the ship considering the morning's success I came up with the title "Operation Argentina" another victory for us.

Museum Review

I cannot help but compare the museum in Buenos Aires with the one in Stanley. This museum is larger, very modern and has several video displays that I cannot put in the book, however, it is lacking in artefacts and is primarily a visual presentation of the Argentine political position. They cannot be getting a large number of visitors and the relatively large number of staff looked disinterested. Perhaps it is different when they get coaches full of children.

Whilst I have been back I have looked at some trip advisor reviews, there are both British and Argentinian ones. As well as the museum is free to enter the guides also did free guided tours but these have been stopped. From some of the English reviews, it was clear that it was not possible to contradict the message that this place portrays and the guides would not accept even the expression of any alternative view.

This museum is a place that reinforces the general indoctrination of the Argentinian people by portraying history that ignores certain important events and even spreads untruths. I cannot establish who paid for the original building or who pays for its upkeep but it is almost certainly the Argentine government and it cannot be cheap to run.

Compare that with the one in Stanley which is crammed full of artefacts and tells the story of the islands from an Islanders point of view, showing all aspects of their life. There is a small section on how the war affected the residents and quite a bit of military hardware which is mostly outside. The assistance I received from the 3 staff during my day-long visit was first class, welcoming and friendly; it is such a shame that they have so much 1982 material that they do not have room to display but that should not put anyone off from visiting.

For me, the visit was very memorable, I am a member of SAMA (South Atlantic Medal Association) which supports veterans of the conflict in many ways such as health mental issues and opportunities to return to the Falklands where we are always made very welcome. They provide the support to all us veterans when we visit this amazing place

I also belong to The Falkland Island Association (FIA) who supports the rights of the islanders to Self Determination which is enshrined in the United Nations charter. Their referendum vote in 2013 was triggered by Argentinian rhetoric and resulted in 99.8% of them voting in favour of remaining a British Overseas Territory. Finding out when the indoctrination started and how is important because it helps me to understand and see the dangers.

That leads me to the conclusion that the conflict between the two countries does not have any possible solution whilst this abhorrent indoctrination continues. One day maybe the Argentine Government will realise the truth and then they could alter their school agenda to include the complete history so that their citizens can make up their minds. Of course, it will take a long time to reverse 79 years of lies but is there any other option, I think not.

My final thought is that the indoctrination in Argentina started in 1934 when Hitler became President of Germany as well as chancellor and in 1941 he invaded Russia. Many Argentinian politicians at the time had pro-fascist views and Hitler was, without doubt, a master of indoctrination. At the end of World War 2, Argentina welcomed many Nazi's because Perón was drawn to fascist ideology and the position we now find ourselves in has routes in these events.

It is now clear to me that we must be always on our guard when dealing with Argentina and that it is very unlikely that they will ever give up their claim; we must be prepared to defend the people who live there as was done in 1982.

Review of the Rattenbach Report

I only found that this document existed because of my trip to the museum and then only after I had translated the information in the museum displays. Luckily the document has been published online by the Argentine government but only in Spanish. I could not find an English version and had to rely on Google translate so that I could read it. Whilst I accept that the translation is not ideal, it was very interesting to read their side of the story.

6 senior officers, two from each service created this report in 1982 under the leadership of General Rattenbach who was appointed by General Galtieri.

The first section includes much of the history of the Argentinian claim for sovereignty, most of which is covered by the previous chapters, however, the following paragraph was included in the early 1970's section where Argentina appeared to be friendly towards the Falklands and was providing support such as supplies and transport. Where I have copied from my Rattenbach Report translation the text is in *italics as here*.

28. Support for the islanders, at first, gave good results, as a way of approaching the idea of the transfer of sovereignty. This good start, however, was clouded by certain difficulties that occurred on the islands when the massive arrival of Argentine tourists in passenger ships began.

The Falkland Islands were going through a difficult time; the population was dwindling and the infrastructure probably could not cope with tourists, especially large groups of Argentinians who believed that they should own this place, no wonder there were problems. No transport, no café's, no souvenir shops and nowhere to visit along with a population who probably didn't trust the visitors or their motives can you blame them?

Today tourism is embraced, cruise ships visit but the volume is limited by physical travel restrictions. Only 50% of ships get passengers ashore because of local weather variability and flights are limited. Even today the few Argentine tourists that do manage to get to the islands appear to cause most of the trouble; it's in their nature because of what they are ALL taught at school.

The document then goes on to discusses the initial phases of negotiations between the UK & Argentina from 1980, the UN negotiations, both pre-war and during along with the Argentinian war planning process.

I am just a "foot soldier" well naval engineer really and have never before considered that these events are planned or that Governments have a structured process that should be followed. No wonder there are so many senior officers.

The military Junta established a Working Party on the 12th Jan 1982 and specified in paragraph 114 that their task was to "*analyze the forecast of the Use of Military Power for the Falklands case, with a military-political approach that specifies the possible modes of action*". They were verbally told to plan for an invasion, even though no formal National Strategy was calling for an invasion which would be the normal first step.

Initial planning was for the invasion to take place later in the year, after we had "demilitarised" our forces which were due to start in May 1982, Galtieri made a grave mistake in bringing the operation date forward. Formal planning for an invasion started approx. 27th Jan 1982 and on 20th March 1982, a decision was taken to invade. The originally planned invasion date was 9th July 1982 and this was later changed to 15th May 1982 with a proviso of no sooner than 1st May 1982.

They were made aware early on in the general peace negotiations that the United States would support the UK if an invasion took place.

The report concludes that if the planning had taken place correctly they would have properly assessed the risks and the whole thing would never have taken place. There was also no plan for evacuation should we despatch a "Task Force". Quote from paragraph 159 of my translated version of Spanish to English, "*When the most dangerous capacity of the enemy, which was to react with all its military might with the support of the US, became effective, there were no contingency plans that foresaw this possibility, which would have provided the strategic-military and political leadership of the Nation to come to a more decent outcome than the one finally obtained.*

When questioned by this Commission, the main military and civil authorities agree in stating that a British reaction with massive use of its military power was considered little less than impossible, at least in the initial stage of planning the Argentine military alternative." They did not think we would come.

Planning for the occupation had not been completed at the time of the invasion, apart from the initial invasion and dealing with any first resistance by forces already on the islands. This probably accounts for the general feeling of the Islanders that the occupation forces did not know what they were doing; they just made it up as they went along.

There was no overall co-ordination between the 3 services for the defence of the island and there was no plan to supply the invasion force plus its residents. Add to that the appointment of a military governor rather than a civilian one who would have been more acceptable to the International community.

Planning for the defence of the islands started 10 days after the invasion which meant that Britain had started planning to recover the islands and despatched a task force before Argentina had any plan to defend them.

The invasion agenda was driven by the activities that were going on in South Georgia just before the invasion, which were the activities of some Argentinian scrap metal merchants. From reading the document, it is clear that this was not a provocation planned by the Argentine government but it was exacerbated by the actions of the civilians involved. There is a dispute as to whether they raised an Argentine flag; however, it is very likely they did because they have all been taught in school that the islands are theirs by right.

From the report:

272. The incident in the South Georgia Islands originated when Argentine personnel landed on the Island, hoisted the national flag - on their own initiative - and did not fulfil the immigration requirements demanded by the British authorities.

273. This fact became the triggering element of the South Atlantic conflict, producing a British reaction considered exaggerated, and precipitating the decision of the Military Junta to bring forward the "Blue" operation

Blue was the Invasion Plan.

274. There is no evidence that the company group "Islas Georgia del Sur SA" has been used by either party to precipitate events, although the Navy intended to take advantage of these private activities to facilitate the settlement of a station, and scientists on South Georgia Island with the approval of the Ministry of the Argentine Foreign Office.

This is proof that the Argentine Navy did intend to take advantage of the scrap metal workers and I suspect that our intelligence services knew this.

In the UK members of the Houses of Parliament who support the Falklands used this activity to try and get the Falklands garrison increased. A small number of Marines were sent south and the Junta, fearing an increase in opposition to a landing which would stop the invasion panicked and invaded.

This all came to head in Argentina on the 16th March 1982 and the invasion planning was hastily completed over the next 4 days.

The actual invasion did follow the plan and was, of course, a success although they did suffer several casualties and the Marines in Stanley did a great job with no casualties.

There is no reference in the document to the situation in Argentina where public opinion had been turning against the Junta; the invasion changed that which must have been a consideration for their decision.

From the 4th April, all written planning activity stopped and the war was conducted by the Military Command structure. On the 7th April, reserve forces were called up as well despite the original plans not requiring this.

Returning to the South Georgia incident the report says:

284. Regarding the capture of the South Georgia Islands, the following can be established:

a. The objective of taking the population of Grytviken was achieved, without causing casualties to the enemy, but at a cost that should be considered excessive (2 dead, 7 wounded, 1 destroyed helicopter and a damaged corvette).

Well done our Marines. Perhaps it was the success of the 2 invasion operations that led them to believe they could defend the islands from our Task Force.

The next few hundred paragraphs consider the peace attempts by Peru and the final UN peace efforts which take place as the Task Force sails south and continue well into the initial engagements of the war.

Peru is a friend of Argentina, probably because they share no borders; South American politics are very complex. The sinking of the Belgrano appears to have scuttled the Peru first attempt from an Argentinian point of view. There is no mention of the Sheffield strike on 5th May but perhaps they think at this stage that they are in a strong military position.

19th May is when the British negotiation position hardens at the UN; we will only accept a withdrawal, the UN continues to try to get Argentina to withdraw.

Peru try for peace again on 20th May but it is rejected by Britain and the landings start in San Carlos, this also allowed Britain to harden its negotiating stance in the UN even more.

The political conclusion of this document is that the Argentine government would have been best served by complying with the UN Resolution 502 which required them to withdraw their troops. Had they done this they would have improved their International standing and negotiations over the Sovereignty of the islands could have restarted. Resolution 502 was British inspired and the Argentine diplomats were wrong-footed by it. They thought that their friends at the UN would support them but they did not, we now had the Right to Self Defence per UN article 51 and so attack.

Paragraph 580

8) The movements of troops of the Armed Forces of Chile in the South affected the deployment of part of our forces in the Theatre of Operations of the South Atlantic, (In the assignment of Army reinforcements to the Falkland Islands, priority was assigned to defence against Chile, which is why they did not send the four regular Infantry Brigades I, M, VI and VIII).

In other words, there was a distinct threat of war on 2 fronts however the Military leadership did not review their strategic plans when this became obvious. Any review would have concluded that they could not hold the islands and should have withdrawn.

ARMY PLANNING

The planning of the troops dispatched to the island did not consider the conditions expected on the islands, the quality of the troops sent or the quality of the forces they would face. Conditions in winter on the islands can be harsh, and then they sent ill-prepared conscripts who would have to face regular soldiers.

NAVY PLANNING

The Commander in Chief of the Navy approved the invasion despite his fleet not being fully operational and ready, he then compounded the error by withdrawing the fleet after the sinking of the Belgrano. Apart from the performance of the naval aircraft from land bases their Navy completely failed.

AIR FORCE PLANNING

The report is quite complimentary about their performance however it is critical in 3 important aspects, they had not practised against naval targets, the bombs were not prepared correctly for the type of target or how they would be used, and finally, they failed to get the materials required to extend the runway to the islands so that they could operate from the Falklands, all vital.

With regards to any British landing, there were no plans to counter this in any way. The Navy Command assumed that the British blockade of the islands was impossible to defeat when in reality there was plenty of scope for ships to sneak past our submarines, just a bit risky, that's all.

657. In aerial combat, there was a clear superiority on the part of the enemy, because the latter had the latest generation missile "SIDEWINDER AIM-9L" provided to Great Britain by the US. The lack of ability to refuel our planes limited their time on the objectives to 2/3 minutes to avoid running out of fuel. Despite this, the enemy did not take advantage of their total or permanent air superiority, since it could not prevent the significant losses inflicted on its surface naval facilities.

We never had total or permanent air superiority until near the end. Most estimates I have seen suggest that they had 10 minutes on the objective and not 2/3 minutes, maybe this was the case for a few missions. The other failing the report misses is that they should have attacked the support ships during the landings but maybe we positioned our warships to discourage that.

658. During the last days of the British advance towards Port Stanley and until the capitulation of our forces, the South Air Force tried to give close fire support by attacking the enemy, who were strongly defended by S/A missiles of the infantry type "RAPIER" and "BLOW PIPE".

This action was not as effective as would have been desirable, due to the strong British anti-aircraft defence, the non-existence of an operational combat line and the inability of our forces to mark the targets. To this must be added the lack of joint training in this and other warlike aspects.

669. It should be mentioned that in the few joint operations between the Argentine Air Force and Naval Aviation, significant successes were achieved, such as the attack on HMS "Invincible", which was successful.

Invincible was never hit; they can't identify their real successes.

677. Regarding the exercise of the functions that were his, it was observed, of General Menéndez, that he thought the tasks of Governor was more important than those of military leadership.

This attitude was seen and condemned by high military authorities who visited the Islands, even before hostilities have begun.

At the same time, tasks of control of the civilian population were neglected, since, through it, the enemy was able to obtain information that was of special importance to them.

The importance of situations outside the defences of Port Stanley was ignored, and he was generally ignorant of the true tactical situation, particularly of the morale and physical condition of the troops detached in these sectors. Thus he confirmed the capitulation of Darwin-Goose Green, without full knowledge of the situation.

The report is quite damming of this man but he was in an almost impossible position, if the original planning had been done properly he should not have been there.

Commander of the Army Component of the Falklands Military Garrison.

687. This Command was initially exercised by the Commander of the IX Infantry Brigade and, was then taken over when they arrived in the Islands, by the Commander of the Mechanized Infantry X Brigade, due to his seniority, from APR 15 82. Command of the Terrestrial Component was by General Jofre the Joint Military Commander.

On 26 MAY 82, General Menéndez issued an Operations Order in which, implicitly, he resumed personal leadership of the Argentine Army stationed in the Islands, restructuring the chain of command in force up to that time. In that order, General Menéndez readjusted the areas of responsibility, the assignment of units, and ordered the III Infantry Brigade Commander to transfer his command post to Darwin.

688. Regarding the deployment of troops, this Commission states:

a. Fox Bay was considered a strong point, and the 8th Infantry Regiment was sent there, an infantry unit without land or air mobility and with limited logistics, with an assigned mission of "Defend Fox Bay, as a point of support, thus controlling the East Falkland Island from there, to prevent Great Britain from conquering important areas of it".

b. Subsequently, that combat element was ordered to help with Darwin's recovery and, together with the 5th Infantry Regiment, operate on the British rear. The situation of these Units, given the isolation to which they were subjected, was already seriously compromised.

c. The suggestion to cover the Port San Carlos area with troops of a certain level was rejected.

d. The proposal to occupy and fortify important heights that were on the way from Darwin to Port Stanley was also rejected, 'heights that were later conquered by the enemy without much effort'.

e. Since the Great Combat Unit did not order the sending of suitable essentials (vehicles, kitchens, etc.), it was forced to use the facilities of other units, creating difficulties for them.

689. Regarding the exercise of command, the important aspects that must be mentioned are:

a. Allowed the landing of San Carlos and later the fall of Darwin, there was no decision to rebuild the defensive structure and orientate the main effort towards the West.

b. As the enemy attack progressed, it was not decided to occupy important heights promptly, and when it was done, the lack of time and adequate resources prevented better preparation and timely defence.

c. The operations were conducted in a strictly personal way, through the radio with overloaded channels, aspects that made the provisions frequently arrive too late.

d. The maintenance of a very small reserve and its inconvenient location prevented flexibility of defence. This resulted in a loss of some favourable opportunities for its use, especially taking into account the progressive loss of helicopters suffered.

e. Did not take advantage of the pleasant success of Bluff Cove, to exploit it tactically with available means.

For those involved in the land battle, you can see from these paragraphs that so much more could have been done to stop us. The report continues after this to say that they should have been better supported from the start.

The land forces commander General Jofre is also lambasted for his authoritarian style which inhibited his subordinates.

I have included this section because I am sure it will interest those involved in these locations, Goose Green & Port Howard:

Commander of III Infantry Brigade.

691. This Brigade moved from the Province of Corrientes, to join the Theatre of Operations of the South Atlantic organization, in anticipation of the southern conflict.

In the third week of April, while organizing the position assigned by the commander of Army Corps V, its Commander was summoned to the City of Commodore Rivadavia, where he was ordered to transfer the Infantry III brigade to the Falklands.

692. The personnel were transported by air and the material was initially planned to be transported by sea, but had to be unloaded from the ship and moved to Falklands by air. Much of their supplies NEVER REACHED THE TROOPS.

693. Immediately after the troops arrived, the structure of the Falklands Military Garrison Command was restructured, putting the 5th Infantry Regiment at Port Howard and the 12th Infantry Regiment at Darwin. Reg. Infantry 4 remained in the vicinity of Port Stanley to complete its equipment and, subsequently, joined the defence of the capital of the Islands.

Reg. Infantry 5 was helo transported in successive flights to its position, with supplies for 5 days and mortars lacking ammunition. Reg. Infantry 12, who received the order to move to Darwin on foot, was also airlifted to their destination, using valuable flight hours which were necessary for more important operational tasks.

694. Regarding the exercise of command, the most salient aspects are:

a. The order was given to Reg. Infantry 5 to go to Port Howard, which would later be called the mission. "The move to that place was also given to a part of the Brigade General Staff and a Military Hospital, this staff having the only means of communications that the III Infantry Brigade had in the Islands.

b. The structured defensive scheme for Darwin Goose Green was extremely weak. The effort required of the troops was greater than their capabilities and was the result of the Brigade Commander's poor knowledge of their general condition and the terrain characteristics, and his absence from his units.

c. The existence of two Commanders in Darwin (BAM Cóndor and Reg. Inf. 12) without the proper assignment of authority made coordinating tasks between the two elements difficult, a circumstance that he knew about because he solved it later. Although this was not his responsibility, it affected a unit of his command.

d. After the Battle of Goose Green, dated 29, it was ordered that the RI 5 troops carry out an operation on East Falkland. After crossing the Strait of San Carlos, for which they had no means they were then to carry out an 8 km march through extremely broken terrain and, reconquer Darwin, which once again revealed his lack of knowledge of the situation of his Brigade. (By this time the field artillery and the troops showed signs of malnutrition).

e. The forces of RI 5, as well as those of RI 12 (Port Howard, Darwin, Goose Green), had serious logistical limitations, lacked vehicles and any assured source of supplies, little ammunition, and their combat capacity was diminished by 40 to 50%.

f. In Darwin's actions, the misuse of helicopters in transport tasks and inadequate formations limited the defence's counterattack ability.

g. Another of the critical elements was the Command of Companies 601 and 602, who were not used in functions consistent with their specialization.

Strange and meaningless missions were assigned to them, which wore them out, and this unnecessarily deprived us of a suitable resource that could have brought concrete and effective benefits.

695. Regarding the exercise of the Command, the following should be highlighted:

a. There was profound ignorance about the status of the forces in the Infantry Brigade III Command, which had its origin not only in the above but also in the absence of the commander, who installed his command post in a house in Port Stanley, where he lived with part of his General Staff security personnel.

b. General Parada only went to the place where his General Staff (Town Hall) was on a few occasions. His style of command meant he did not properly consider his General Staff's advice.

c. When he was given the order to transfer his command post to Darwin (May 26), he did not complete this move, which prevented him from being present in the Darwin Goose Green battles. On that occasion, he directed the operations of the Unit that defended the sector, by radio, and subsequently confirmed the decision of the head of Task Force CEDES "to surrender his forces.

d. He did not comply with his appointment as Delegate commissioner, Governor for the West Falkland, this was his only area of responsibility and he did not attend even once.

e. In Port Stanley, the Brigade Commander did very little and did not contribute to the action of the Great Combat Unit.

f. The personal characteristics of the Infantry Brigade III Commander were decisive factors in his inadequate performance.

There were small groups of other services covered in the report which also make for interesting reading:

National Gendarmerie is the Border Guards

697. The National Gendarmerie was present in the conflict in the South Atlantic, with the dispatch of 40 men belonging to its security force.

698. The aforementioned personnel joined the Command Company where they had a notable attitude and incurred casualties in combat action against the enemy.

Argentine Naval Prefecture is the Coastguard

699. After the recovery of the Falkland Islands, on 02-APR-82 the Argentina Naval Prefecture sent, personnel and suitable means for:

a. organize and implement the maritime police services per the provisions of laws 18,398 and 18,771.

b. Study the settlement of the future Prefecture and its features.

700. For this reason, the Coast Guard GC 82 "FALKLAND ISLANDS" and GC 83 "IGUAZÚ RIVER", Short Skyvan PA-50 and PA-54 aircraft, and the PUMA PA-12 helicopter were sent to the archipelago.

701. Given the prevailing situation in the Islands and as the various events unfolded, these outstanding units, especially the surface units, carried out countless activities, with complete efficiency and demonstrated their capabilities.

702. The activities carried out were:

Pilotage, transportation of personnel, material and ammunition, reconnaissance, radar picket activities, patrols, communications interception, and exploration flights, logistical and operational flights (Search And Rescue).

703. *Their most outstanding activities were:*

a. Bypass the blockade imposed by the British, carried out by the two coast guards vessels on their journey from the mainland to the archipelago, on April 12.

b. Repulse the attack of two enemy Sea Harrier aircraft on GC-83 "RÍO IGUAZÚ" on MAY 22.

c. Endure, despite the lack of suitable weapons, other attacks in which personnel were killed by enemy fire.

Aerial Observer Network. Mainly Amateurs

704. *The Argentine Air Force, faced with the need to extend the scope of detection and control of airspace, and to cover the radio shadow cones caused by the terrain, created an Aerial Observer Network. This was done mainly with a group of volunteer radio amateurs who regularly did this work in times of peace. They did not hesitate to assist, giving proven signs of sacrifice, disregard and courage. Sitting in their Aerial Observer Posts, in the middle of the combat zone they raised the alarm in time for the defence. This network was completed with military personnel. Its silent and effective action under rigorous climatic and combat conditions thus allowed the increase of operations of the Falkland Islands air defence.*

The Phoenix Squad

705. *In any conflict or war, problems must be solved that result from the unpredictability of or lack of capability, which forces the taking of quick resolutions to correct those shortcomings. Thus they created and added to the South Air Force Command a group that was later named "Phoenix Squad", which amalgamated civil and military crews in the same spirit of service to carry out assigned mission. The aforementioned squadron was made up of requisitioned civil aircraft, of the Lear Jet and FA type, which, despite not having been designed for war purposes, deserved the recognition and appreciation of the commanders and members of the Argentine Air Force for the work done.*

706. They carried out such tasks as in-flight refuelling, light transport, exploration and reconnaissance, search and rescue, false missions (to confuse the enemy and keep them on permanent alert) and guidance of combat squadrons to the vicinity of the objective, being able to make these last two look like real combat missions.

707. They did this without complaint and when an FA Lear Jet was shot down by a Sea Dart missile, during a scouting mission, they gave their quota of blood.

No mention here of the second Learjet pilot who saw his buddy shot down and bailed out, leaving his passengers to their fate, a Seadart missile was on its way to him but detonated mid-flight due to a technical fault in the Seadart system. It is believed that the plane with passengers crashed and the pilot did not survive.

Auxiliary Ships

708. During the operations of the South Atlantic, supply ships of the Navy were used, mainly in logistical tasks. The activities carried out by them were as follows:

a. Oil tankers "Campo Durán" and "Puerto Rosales", in refuelling tasks for the Units of the Sea Fleet.

b. ELMA Transport "Córdoba", was loaded in Mar del Plata with AA and ground artillery material for the Army, set sail for the South and was diverted to Puerto Deseado, not crossing to the Islands.

ELMA "Formosa", made a single trip from Buenos Aires to Port Stanley before the exclusion zone was established, remained in Port Stanley due to unloading problems until May 1, when it sailed suffering air attacks.

ELMA "Río Carcarañá" circumvented the blockade imposed by the enemy by transporting material to the troops in the Islands. On April 26, it arrived in Port Stanley. After it's unloading, it was sent to the Falkland Sound for logistical support of the West Falkland, where it was destroyed by enemy action, on May 16.

c. On APR 29 Tug "Yehuin" transported flat-topped barges for the transports to unload onto; this was due to the problems caused in unloading due to the precariousness of the port facilities in Port Stanley, arriving at the Islands on MAY 01.

709. The tasks carried out by the majority of the crews of the listed ships and others showed the preparation, efficiency and spirit of sacrifice of the Argentine merchant seaman.

710. It should be noted that after the recovery of the Falklands, the naval station in Port Stanley was taken over and manned. Small enemy ships, including Forrest, Penepe and Monsunenm, which they manned and maintained an active role until the end of the conflict, navigating between the coves of the Islands, and accomplished among others, patrol functions, logistical support and troop transport.

Commercial Aviation

711. Given the need to increase the volumes of cargo and passengers to be transported to the Falkland Islands, the Argentine Air Force partially mobilized commercial means belonging to Aerolineas Argentinas and Austral.

712. Between 02 and 03-APR, the personnel involved from both companies carried out an enthusiastic and effective action that assisted the Air Bridge in the mission of deploying and supplying our troops in the Falkland Islands.

As I have read through the final stages of the war, I wonder if the authors have ever been to the islands, or if any of the planners had as well. There was some intelligence carried out before the invasion because intelligence officers visited the islands beforehand, but whatever they took back was useless.

The next section considers Logistic support and makes interesting reading, especially the effect on moral; I know that our Armed Forces are nothing without our support services which are the best in the world.

Logistics

724. As a fundamental and synthesizing aspect, initially consider the content of point 4. SUPPORTS OF DEMIL NO 1/82, which is, the governing document prepared by the strategic military leadership:

4 SUPPORT

The necessary Annexes corresponding to the different support requirements had been omitted, to enable the maximum secrecy of the operation.

It can be seen, then, that in light of this report that there was never going to be coherence in logistics planning activities.

The principle that governs the logistics functions: "Provide to provide" was completely distorted.

Technical and logistical difficulties and deficiencies.

725. *With this first concept stated, the paragraphs that follow are intended to consider the technical and logistical difficulties and deficiencies related to the action of the proper forces in the execution of war operations. It is convenient to highlight, initially, two considerations:*

a. In a general frame of reference, we can establish that the degree of technical capacity of our forces was substantially less than that of the enemy. This difference was less with teams of a high level of technical ability and professional personnel. It was extraordinarily greater in non-professional personnel, and especially those with basic equipment and weapons.

The main experiences and lessons refer to the specific tactical field, so this Commission will limit itself to making the global statement of major technical deficiencies.

b. As stated in previous chapters, component logistics was the responsibility of each force. It is difficult, for the time being, to indicate, as in the technical aspects, the logistical difficulties in a generalized way.

Due to these circumstances, this Commission has decided to consider the logistical difficulties and deficiencies, EXCLUSIVELY AS REGARDS THE LOGISTIC SUPPORT OF THE FALKLANDS MILITARY GARRISON.

Technical deficiencies

726.

a. Individual team

The individual equipment available was not, due to its characteristics, the most suitable for the environmental conditions of the area. The impossibility of carrying out adequate maintenance (washing, repairing, disinfecting), due to the scarcity of equipment and facilities, decreased their useful life and performance and considerably affected the health and mental state of the troops.

b. Individual and small-scale weapons (rifles, machine guns, mortars, recoilless cannons and rocket launchers.)

In a large number of cases, the corresponding provisions did not reach the users. The maintenance carried out was deficient. The ammunition provisions were, in many cases, insufficient.

c. Field artillery (The deficiencies respond to the full employment of the Artillery, regardless of the sector where the error, shortcoming, etc., originates, which causes it). In general, it can be established that the artillery available, although of outstanding performance, was not, due to its limitations, the most suitable for use in the Islands.

The most important deficiencies were:
1) Difficulties in locating targets.
2) Difficulties in achieving adequate mobility.
3) Difficulties in evaluating the results of the firing.

The Royal artillery provided Fire Support Teams for all British Forces doing the above work. Along with signal support from naval ratings they ensured that the Royal Navy Naval Gun Fire Support (NGFS) was as effective as possible. These teams were amongst the busiest squads in the war,

4) Our Artillery had a shorter range than enemy Artillery, except for 3 in No 155 mm calibre pieces, which were belatedly required and shipped.

d. Night combat

It is in this activity, where our forces have shown the main technical deficiencies. This was further evidenced by the high technical ability shown by the enemy.

e. Aero mobility

This is one of the fields in which the inferiority was most notable. Added to this was the failure to obtain local air superiority and the enemy's anti-aircraft capacity.

f. Rationing

There were deficiencies in the preparation of food and its distribution, which negatively affected the physical and emotional state of the troops. (Major Ceballos's Medical Statement).

Argentina sent 12 field kitchens to the Falklands, only two of them used petrol for fuel, the rest were wood burning in a land of no trees. They may have used local peat for fuel but I doubt it would be very effective.

Logistical difficulties and deficiencies

727. As stated in the introduction, it is difficult to try to include in this subchapter all the logistical deficiencies detected in each of the Armed Forces and in the different places where different elements operated. It is for this reason that recourse is made, as a synthesis, to the logistical deficiencies and difficulties detected in supporting the Argentine troops that fought on the islands.

There was a great difference between the actual logistical capacity of the Armed Forces and the development of this capacity concerning the elements highlighted in Port Stanley. This great difference consisted of TRANSPORT. (Annex VII / 17).

Deficiencies at the national level

728.

a. A PEN Decree was issued so that before and during war operations, companies both state and private organizations were in a position to compulsorily satisfy the requirements of the Armed Forces at all times.

b. The weakness of the national organization, the lack of a railway and road infrastructure plus facilities for operational requirements. The inadequacy of the infrastructure in the cargo terminals, given their probable use by the Forces (loading and unloading ramp), were noted, especially for armoured vehicles with their corresponding accessories and auxiliary material, etc.

In other words, they were unable to send heavy armour.

c. In the south of the country, there were problems, both for the supply of class II and III effects (fuels and lubricants for vehicles and aircraft) in drums, and their shipment to Falklands, having to be transported from Buenos Aires because Comodoro Rivadavia did not have a bottled plant.

Deficiencies at the military level
729.
a. As regards the application of the Joint Logistics Doctrine, there was evidence of a lack of coordination of efforts, especially of the supply and transportation, so it is convenient to review it to facilitate joint logistical management (Example: common use, compatible communications equipment, etc.).

b. Transport by air, which was carried out with great risk and until the last moment, was not sufficient to provide the minimum supply needs of the troops stationed in the Islands.

We knew that a Hercules arrived daily and were unable to stop it but its contribution was a drop in the ocean.

The deficiencies at the operational level
730.
a. The lack of knowledge of the Strategic Military Directive by the responsible elements resulted in the lack of elaboration of the corresponding Logistics Support Plan, leaving everything partly subject to improvisation.

b. Item 4. LOGISTICS of the COATLANSUR Schematic Plan No. 1/82 "S" stated:

"4 LOGISTICS

Logistics support will be the responsibility of each component group in Falklands, with this Command coordinating through the Military Commander."

"The logistical support of the rest of the units that are required will be the responsibility of each force."

"Logistical support to the civilian population will be the responsibility of the economic area, in coordination with the Military Government."

As it appears from the reading of this section, the forecasts of the TOAS Command, regarding logistics, cannot be considered profound and responsible.

A brief check of what has been stated could be to try to answer the following question:

The TRANSPORT of materials is a logistical function. How would the Army satisfy the needs of the component of its Force that made up *the Falklands Military Command, in a THEATRE OF OPERATIONS with aircraft?*

Obviously, in three simple paragraphs and without a logistical annexe, questions of this nature could not be satisfied, when it was known that the problem was not to obtain materials but to transport them.

c. Given the characteristics of the area and the distance to the large supplier centres, it was necessary to have in advance an adequate infrastructure for the storage and formation of the deposits, concerning the future use of the Forces.

Britain has huge stores filled with WAR STORES and it is the availability of these stores that allowed the despatching of the Task Force in record time.

Final conclusions
731.

a. The technical inferiority of our troops to the enemy is evident. Much of it could have been lessened, had conscious and timely preparation been made for conflict.

b. The greatest technical deficiencies were found in the Army personnel, derived from the fact that a large part of the troop had very little training time.

c. Technical means and other equipment had to be acquired during the conflict, which made their costs higher.

d. Much equipment and materials could not reach the users, due to the development of the situation, while others came too late.

e. THE NATIONAL PREPARATION FROM THE LOGISTIC POINT OF VIEW WAS DEFICIENT.

f. IN THE LOGISTIC FIELD IT CANNOT BE IMPROVISED. In these circumstances, we proceeded and suffered the consequences.

g. Operations plans did not develop logistical functions in acceptable detail.

h. DEFICIENCIES IN TRANSPORT PREVENTED THE NORMAL DELIVERY OF SUPPLIES.

The section about support is one of the main reasons that they lost and our support was the reason we won, lack of support costs lives as well as the war.

Psychological management.

732. Given the great influence that psychological management had during and after the conflict, by both our country and the United Kingdom, the Evaluation Commission has carried out work on this important field of human action.

733. Said work is included as Annexes VII / 18 and VII / 19, and its conclusions are as follows:

a. When the conflict began, there was no adequate organization in the country for the direction, intelligence, planning, execution and evaluation of psychological management.

b. There were also no national definitions regarding the complex issues of Social Communication and Psychological Management.

c. The most suitable body, the Ministry of Public Information, was not adequately exploited, despite having an organization and equipment that, although not ideal, were the most adaptable to the current situation.

d. The organization that had primary responsibility in the matter, without having experience, was the Joint Chiefs of Staff. It had only a basic organization for the execution of the tasks, which had to be done urgently and the conflict had already started.

e. The time aspect, so important in this activity, aggravated this failure.

In psychological management, everything had to be improvised. Errors and successes were subject to the discretion of the managers, who had to execute the work without the support of efficient prior planning.

f. All the agencies linked to psychological management depended on the Armed Forces and others at a national level. They were gradually separated from their work because priority was given to internal politics.

g. Main errors

1) Lack of an adequate organization at a higher level, that would have implemented a National System of Social Communication.

2) Lack of a sufficient number of military specialists in this complex field of command support.

3) Lack of knowledge, discontent and even excessive caution regarding the use of terminology and the implementation of measures related to psychological management.

4) Inadequate use of the available means.

5) Inefficient information control, which provided valuable data for the enemy.

6) An excessively permissive environment regarding the handling of information during the war, which allowed some journalistic overflows with multiplying triumphalist effects on the internal public.

7) Difficulties in the centralized conduct of Psychological management because of multiple interferences by the different Armed Forces.

8) Lack of adaptation of the guidelines to changes in the situation, which led to the execution of an outdated and negative Psychological management, especially during the final phase of the conflict.

h. Qualification of the psychological management cycle

1) Management phase

This phase began after the occupation of the Islands was carried out and, therefore, lost its forecast meaning.

2) Intelligence Phase

It could not be carried out previously due to the secrecy imposed on the operation. We then resorted to basic intelligence, voluminous and outdated, to respond to an unprecedented situation. Intelligence during the conflict addressed only the conjectural.

3) Planning Phase

It was not carried out previously, for the same reason.

4) Execution Phase

It was developed with enthusiasm and dedication but without adequate knowledge.

There was no coordination in the use of the media, and control was poor. The partial evaluation, tending to produce partial modifications and was not carried out adequately.

5) Evaluation Phase
It is appreciated that this phase had not been fully developed, but must be to gain experience for the future.

Psychological management (propaganda) is now part of a modern war situation; it was the British press that informed the Argentinians that their bombs were not exploding. What the authors of the report do not take into account is the effects of the indoctrination that has been going on all this time. From a public point of view once they had invaded there was no going back.

Chapter VIII - The causes of defeat
Conclusion
764. The procedures adopted by the Military Junta led the Nation to war without adequate preparation. By contradicting essential planning norms they generated fundamental errors and omissions that affected the military strategy and the coherence of planning. All this constituted a decisive cause of defeat.

786. As the planned date for the execution of Operation Blue was brought forward, the following inconveniences occurred:

a. The equipping of the Armed Forces had not yet been completed. As an example, the Super Etendard-Exocet material that was left on the quays of Marseille deserves to be highlighted, as it was hit by an embargo on arms exports by France, shortly before shipment to the country.

This is proof that the French did support us, they had ordered 14 Super Etendard Jets and 15 Air launched Exocet. At the start of the war, they only had 5 jets and 5 missiles that had been delivered.

b. The Armed Forces were not given time to adequately prepare and train their troops. The Army had not completed the withdrawal of the 1962 class and had just incorporated the 1963 class.

c. The worst time of the year was chosen in terms of its climatic conditions since our troops were not properly equipped or trained to withstand a prolonged siege on the islands. It was also the worst season to allow the Air Force to operate properly (a few hours of daylight, low ceilings, fog, rain, etc.).

790. Because of what is detailed in the preceding chapters, the Commission considers that the members of the Military Junta, the supreme organ of the State (Statute for the Process of National Reorganization, Article) are responsible for:

a. LEADING THE NATION TO WAR WITH GREAT BRITAIN, WITHOUT FULL PREPARATION FOR A CONFRONTATION OF THESE CHARACTERISTICS AND MAGNITUDE WITH THE CONSEQUENCES OF FAILING TO ACHIEVE THE POLITICAL OBJECTIVE AND PLACING THE COUNTRY IN A CRITICAL ECONOMIC AND SOCIAL POLITICAL SITUATION.

798. Notwithstanding the foregoing, it should be noted that this Commission received a complaint along with documentation that links Dr Nicanor Costa Méndez with multinational companies. Since it is already filed, separately, in the Federal Justice, the Honourable Military Junta was informed in due course.

803. The possible irregularity committed in the domain of the Banco de la Nación Argentina and, consequently, within the scope of his ministerial responsibility, was the transfer of official deposits from London to Switzerland, which has already been brought to the attention of the authorities.

Proof that some of the government of Argentina were corrupt at that time; the Junta was by now tearing itself apart and looking for scapegoats for their failure.

The next section lists all the relevant Senior Officers and identifies failures in command charges. Listing these is of no relevance to this document as all the failures have been identified in previous paragraphs.

The final section of the report compares the UK forces combined effort with that of the Argentinian forces.

871. In modern warfare, only the joint integration of the Armed Forces allows the achievement of the proposed military objectives. This requires, therefore, a harmonious, balanced and rational development adapted to the needs of modern combat of the three Armed Forces. It is useless for a force to acquire a certain potential or capacity if it is not accompanied by a similar development in the other forces. Britain demonstrated this by building an amphibious task force perfectly balanced with operational needs. For example, it would have been useless for him to have more warships if the number of planes he transferred to the Theatre of Operations were not sufficient or vice versa. The same can be said of its infantry or artillery.

874. *This has been the only warlike conflict in the Nation so far this century. While peace is a permanent national goal of any civilized community, it is achieved through adequate preparation to deter potential enemies from using force against them.*

875. *Our Armed Forces demonstrated the following weaknesses in the conflict:*

a. Deficiencies in joint action, as mentioned previously.

b. Lack of balanced and harmonious development of the equipment of each Force, subject to the needs of modern warfare and existing war hypotheses.

c. Lack of adequate underwater force.

d. Lack of modern aviation for warfare on land and at sea, and adequate means of exploration and reconnaissance.

e. Lack of professionally updated ground forces, especially for combat in hours of darkness.

f. Lack of organized logistics and conducted with joint criteria.

g. Lack of diverse sources for obtaining weapons and adequate capacity for self-sufficiency, due to the absence of technology and sufficient war industries.

h. Lack of sufficient training in the Armed Forces for the comprehensive use of electronics in all areas of modern warfare (Air, water, land).

Chapter XV - Final conclusions

Last conclusions

879. *The effects resulting from the total blockade of the Islands by Great Britain characterized the situation and the performance of our land forces stationed there. They decisively affected the possibilities of any adequate reinforcement, of the maintenance of those there and any tactical action of combat against the enemy. Finally, they limited almost totally, the transportation of supplies from the mainland to the Islands - thus despite the arduous effort that meant the maintenance of*

the airlift, they imposed serious logistical restrictions that affected our combat capability.

The Rattenbach report is over 105,000 words plus annexes and would merit a book on its own if I had the translation skills.

It is very damning of their efforts and may give the impression after reading all this that this was an easy war for the British, it wasn't easy at all and it could have been much harder.

My final comment concerns the troops that landed in The Falklands, a body of men who had been longing to own these islands all their life because that is what they have been taught.

Few of them would ever have considered what the place was like and would be thrilled to be involved. As time passes for them whilst they wait in miserable cold conditions with little shelter and poor food their moral would have plummeted as they waited for the British. They probably expected the inhabitants to welcome them with open arms as liberators, how wrong they were.

By the time they return home, maybe some of them will understand that The Falklands can only be owned by those who live there and perhaps they will then question why they have been taught as they were.

Puerto Madryn

Puerto Madryn is like the Falklands a wildlife haven but the general topography is somewhat different being arid and dry with less wind and warmer. On my day trip to the nature reserve, we passed their Falklands memorial which is on the seafront quite close to the pier which allowed me to visit it later in the day.

The entrance from the shore road has three large displays that can be seen on the left of this picture.

1   3   2

1. The invisibles
We're not seen coming,
the invisibles,
they crossed the city in the early morning,
in closed trucks like coffins,
they were silenced by an icy drizzle.
No one expected them,
dead or imprisoned,
the little invisible soldiers were a distant chimera.
The people sensed it, they knew it...
behind the olive curtains,
a sob was heard like birds,
bread and blankets,
hugs and claps emerged from the houses.
People dared,
opened the field trucks and found lead
soldiers that were bleeding.
Zita Solari

2. 1982 - June – 2012
today as yesterday the people receive them as heroes

3. The Falkland Islands are Argentinian

1. The conflict

In the early morning of April 2, 1982, Argentine troops that were part of "Operation Rosario", landed in the Falkland Islands, achieving the surrender of British troops who from 1833 had usurped that portion of our territory starting the war that will last for seventy-four days.

During the same, the sinking of the ARA Cruiser General Belgrano, the flight of the Air Force Hawks (FFAA) - Goose Green - Tumbledown - Mt. Longdon - G.C. Iguazu River - Alacrán Squadron of National Gendarmerie are symbols of surrender and self-denial marked by the courage of our soldiers. On 14 June the British entered Port Stanley, managing to silence the voice of the rifles, but not the clamour of our legitimate rights.

"THE ARGENTINE NATION RATIFIES ITS LEGITIMATE AND IMPRESCRIPTIBLE SOVEREIGNTY OVER THE SOUTH GEORGIA ISLANDS AND SOUTH SANDWICH AND THE MARITIME AND ISLAND SPACES OF THE NATIONAL TERRITORY..."

NATIONAL CONSTITUTION ARGENTINA
First Transitory Provision

2. The return home

On June 19, 1982, the British ocean liner "Canberra" tied up at the Almirante Storni Pier in Puerto Madryn, where more than 4,000 Argentine fighters arrived. On June 21, 2000 Argentines arrived in Puerto Madryn aboard the British ship "Norland" and on the 26th, another 577 troops aboard the icebreaker "Almirante Irizar".

Without rifles, with applause, tears and emotion, the people of Madryn offered their love and thanks to the young Argentine soldiers who were transferred to the former Barraca Lahusen where they were sheltered in the first moments of their return to the country.

Through an operation in which the living forces of the town participated, the soldiers received warmth, food and animated support to go through such a difficult historical moment.

There are innumerable anecdotes, stories and stories of Madryn residents who received these heroes in their homes who had left everything on the battlefield and hoped, after so much suffering, to receive affection and contention.

3. The remembrance

As the Twenty-First Anniversary of War Veteran's Day and the Fallen in Falklands was commemorated a Monument reminiscent of the feat was inaugurated.

It consists of a circular fountain of fourteen meters of circumference built in concrete, perimeter wall 80 centimetres high in slab stone, where the plates with the names of the fallen and the shields of each province were placed and on a plane raised to 2 meters sit the images of the Falkland Islands from which the images are raised to natural size, made by the local sculptor José Luis Hamzé.

The figures represent three soldiers, one of them with the national flag and the other holding a fallen one in his arms. The property also consists of a parking promenade with different routes and a mast to fly the national flag.

The people of Madryn received them with open arms and would shelter them eternally in their hearts.

Homage to the heroes who arrived in Puerto Madryn, 30 years ago, after defending the Homeland in the warlike conflict in the Falkland Islands.

June 18, 1982
Mayor Dr. Victoriano Salazar
June 18, 2012

Mayor Ricardo Daniel Sastre

Queen Victoria in the background, on the side of the monument, is a picture of ARA General Belgrano.

The face of the memorial, there is a picture of an A4 Skyhawk on the other side.

THE LANDING – 1982

On June 19, 1982, the British liner "Canberra" moored to the "Almirante Storni" dock, where 4,000 Argentine fighters arrived. On June 21, 2000 Argentines arrived in Puerto Madryn aboard the British ship "Northland" and on the 26th, another 577 troops aboard the icebreaker "Almirante Irizar".

Without rifles, with applause, tears and emotion, the people of Madrid offered their affection and gratitude to the young Argentine soldiers who were transferred to the former Barraca Lahusen who sheltered them in the first moments of their return to the country.

The Madrynazo is an event that these people should be ashamed of, the following diary of events was on another board.

MADRYNAZO for identity and collective memory Municipal Ordinance 6965/08

Municipality of Puerto Madryn - Deliberative Council of Puerto Madryn

Friday 7:
There appears in the Jornada de Trelew newspaper, a story that tells of the arrival in Puerto Madryn of the US fleet that comes from participating in Operation Unitas XXV and that in this city it would carry out restoring tasks.

Saturday 8:
8:00 pm: A group of residents read a proclamation of repudiation of the intention to anchor in Puerto Madryn while a basketball game is held in the municipal gym.

10 pm: A large group of settlers meet; who as the Multisector Commission summons the general population and communicates with the Deliberative Council and express their intention to mobilize to reject the presence of the ships of the United States Navy.

Sunday 9:
10 am: In a radio journalistic program, through LU 17 Radio Puerto Madryn, members of the brand-new multisector commission communicate to the people of Madryn the decision to demonstrate and invite them to participate in it.

12 noon: Approximately one hundred people gathered in the plaza of Puerto Madryn in front of the municipal building, and decide to start a propaganda campaign and carry out a mobilization on Monday at 6:00 p.m. with departure from the plaza to the dock.

6 pm: The Honourable Deliberative Council meets in session with the presence of a huge number of public and unanimously of the three blocks that comprise it (PJ, PACH AND UCR) expresses in its

Declaration that it strongly repudiates the presence of ships in national waters and declares they do not welcome their presence.

Monday 10:
The radio station Sique follows the development of events and calls for the mobilization. A pronouncement of the provincial government is expected.

5 pm: The residents of Madryn begin to meet in front of the Municipality.

5.30 pm: A caravan of vehicles arrives from the neighbouring city of Trelew that travels to the port city to give their support to the community movement.

6 pm: The column leaves for the Almirante Storni Pier, five kilometres from the city.

6.30 pm: The head of the column arrives at the access doors to the port jetty, where they are received by a huge number of protesters who were waiting there along with the pottery workers. The column that arrives counts more than fifteen hundred people.

6:45 pm: A number that far exceeds two thousand protesters pass the checkpoint of the Maritime National Prefecture and heads decisively towards the "US Thorn" that is moored at site 2 of the pier and has started the tasks of loading.

6.55 pm: The head of the column arrived at the place where the ship is anchored. Raising anti-imperialist slogans they force the crew into a small area and the work stops.

7.00 pm: Attempts are made to force them back with jets of water under pressure from the deck of the American ship. Because of this, the crowd responds by throwing objects of all kinds that further expedite the departure tasks. US flags are burned.

7.05 pm: The ship quickly moves away from the jetty in the middle of the popular uproar. On her side is written different phrases in spray, among which is read "Yankees go home".

7.05 pm: Along with the trucks of the protesters, two trucks carrying victuals are removed. There remains a guard of dock workers who continue in a boycott attitude. It is agreed that the city's Volunteer Firefighters will sound their sirens if another mooring is attempted by the ship - which is already about 1,500 meters from the dock - to communicate to the population that it must mobilize again.

19:20 The protesters begin to withdraw in an orderly manner. A group of protesters remains in a state of a vigil that receives the assistance of the community who bring them blankets, coffee and above all solidarity throughout the night.

Tuesday 11
During the morning the community celebrates in the Plaza San Martin the success of the mobilization.
Madryn has won her battle.
Madrynazo 25th Anniversary.
for Identity and Collective Memory.
1984- September 10- 2009.

(This must have been quite a shock for those on the ship, being made welcome in port is something sailors look forward to.

A chance to stretch your legs outside the confines of a steel box, have a drink meet some locals even be invited to someone's house is the norm.

To treat visitors in this way is appalling and the local authorities did nothing, they didn't even try, yet another indication of the mind of most Argentinians, even in a place like this which is a small holiday resort used to welcoming visitor.)

Ushuaia

(This is the central point of this quite large memorial with flag flying and looking out over the harbour.)

(There is a wall to the right with the names of all the fallen.)

(Around the outer footpath is numerous pictures telling the story of the war, underneath the words are in Spanish American and German which probably reflects the nationality of the many cruise ship visitors.)

1   2

1   THE ISLAND OF GOOD MEMORY

Mother, I'm going to the Island
I don't know who to fight
Maybe I will fight, I will resist
or maybe I will die there

What will I do with the uniform
when they start fighting
with the helmet and with the boots
for the same loneliness

Since I came to the Island
I do not have anyone to talk to
we are thousands united
for the same loneliness

And the shots are heard
between death and freedom
my booming body falls
I can't sing anymore

I think it's very cold around here
there is more fear like mine in the city

There is no evil that does not have a name
There is no God to pray to
There are no brothers or soldiers
And there are no judges or juries

There is only one more war
and there is less and less peace
Alejandro Lerner

2   **BACK TO FALKLANDS**

Without hatred or rancour, with courage,
raising the flag of the Fatherland

We will arrive firmly at our islands
that the pirates usurped one day.

Our anger is beating in the wind
there where I roar the shrapnel yesterday,
mowing the lives of so many young people
that the way of return points us.

Our dead dear to Falklands
from their graves they keep custody ...
for them, we will return, for their example,
by the sacrifice of His shed blood.

The sky that is also Argentine
already made the blue and white flag.

Pablo B. Rodrigue

ISLAS MALVINAS

Informamos a nuestros visitantes que, por ley Nacional Argentina N° 26.552 las Islas Malvinas, Georgias del Sur, Sandwich del Sur y los espacios marítimos circundantes, así como el Territorio Antártico Argentino han sido incluidos en la jurisdicción de la Provincia de Tierra del Fuego.

Al mismo tiempo deseamos recordar que las Islas Malvinas, Georgias del Sur, Sandwich del Sur, y los espacios marítimos circundantes se encuentran sometidos desde 1833, a la ocupación ilegal del Reino Unido de Gran Bretaña e Irlanda del Norte.

We inform our visitors that by the Argentine National Law N° 26.552, the Malvinas, South Georgias, South Sandwich Islands and the surrounding maritime areas as well as the Argentine Antarctic Territory, have been included in the jurisdiction of the Province of Tierra del Fuego.

At the same time we should remember that the Malvinas, South Georgias, South Sandwich Islands, and the surrounding maritime areas, are, since 1833, under the illegal occupation of the United Kingdom of Great Britain and Northern Ireland.

ANTÁRTIDA

La República Argentina tiene un sector Antártico en el que su presencia es ininterrumpida desde el año 1904. La Provincia cuenta con una posición geográfica privilegiada. La ciudad de Ushuaia, considerada una de las puertas de acceso a la Antártida, recibe cada temporada casi el 90% del turismo mundial antártico.

Cabe destacar que el Gobierno de la Provincia prioriza el desarrollo y puesta en práctica de programas de cooperación internacional, articulados con el Gobierno Nacional en función de nuestra política de estado provincial en materia antártica y de las políticas orientadas a la consecución de los objetivos del Tratado Antártico.

The Argentine Republic holds an Antarctic Sector, where it has an uninterrupted presence since 1904. The Province of Tierra del Fuego has a privileged geographical position, and every season the city of Ushuaia -held as one of the gateways to Antarctica- receives almost 90% of the tourists that travel from all over the world to Antarctica.

It is noteworthy that the government of the Province prioritizes the development and practice of programs of international cooperation, which are coordinated with the national government and are in consonance with our provincial policies regarding Antarctica and with those policies directed towards the achievement of the goals set in the Antarctic Treaty.

(Ushuaia attitude in all its glory posted next to the Port Gates.)

Author's other books

After the inconclusive Battle of Jutland in World War 1, German U-boats wreaked havoc on our merchant ships, and salvage of both ships and cargoes became of vital importance. Amongst these, Royal Fleet Auxiliary Racer and her riggers recovered U-boat UC-44 together with many documents, including her crucial and secret radio codebook.

Anthony Babb's research has now established that this was used by Bletchley Park's predecessor Room 40, to decode their messages and inform the Admiralty of German submarine movements, changing the course of the war.

U-Boat Enigmas is both a novel and a reference book, including many photographs collected by Able Seaman John Foulkes RNR who served at the Battle of Jutland and in RFA Racer.

The book provides a fascinating new insight into how the salvage riggers and Room 40 saved Britain in WW1.

Anthony Babb BEM

SOUTH AMERICAN WILDLIFE

Queen Victoria 2020 Cruise

Wildlife and cruising are natural companions; ships attract the animals for both food and interaction.

Passengers walk the decks for exercise or are out in the sun and fresh air. Seeing a whale is on most people's agenda and they like to know what the species are. Any sighting is treated by most as an enhancement of the holiday whatever the species and quality pictures help with identification.

This is a record from the Queen Victoria trip in 2020 which was a complete circumnavigation of South America including a trip up the Amazon, where I spent many hours photographing and identifying what I saw. Each photograph has notes to provide information on what was seen giving useful facts and quite often identification tips.

Whether you took this trip, another such trip or even a part of such a voyage, it is a memento of your trip and a guide to many of the species that you could have seen.

The book will also provide those who are thinking about a trip like this some idea of what can be seen.

The Author

Anthony Babb served for 23 years in the Royal Navy as a Weapons System engineer and was awarded the British Empire Medal in the 1988 New Year's Honours list for services to the Royal Navy.

Since retiring he has lectured on cruise ships many times, his first lecture was presented on the P & O ship Oriana in 2012.

He is a 1982 Falklands veteran, a member of SAMA, The South Atlantic Medal Association and a member of the FIA, Falkland Islands Association.